LEARNING
FROM
OUR
MISTAKES

A Reinterpretation
of Twentieth-Century
Educational Theory

HENRY J. PERKINSON

CONTRIBUTIONS TO THE STUDY OF
EDUCATION, NUMBER 14
Greenwood Press
WESTPORT, CONNECTICUT · LONDON, ENGLAND

Library of Congress Cataloging in Publication Data

Perkinson, Henry J.
    Learning from our mistakes.

    (Contributions to the study of education, ISSN 0196-
707X ; no. 14)
    Bibliography: p.
    Includes index.
    1. Education—Philosophy—History—20th century.
I. Title. II. Series.
LA132.P39 1984   370'.1   83-26670
ISBN 0-313-24239-9 (lib. bdg.)

Library of Congress Catalog Card Number: 83-26670
ISBN: 0-313-24239-9
ISSN: 0196-707X

First published in 1984

Greenwood Press
A division of Congressional Information Service, Inc.
88 Post Road West, Westport, Connecticut 06881

Printed in the United States of America

10 9 8 7 6 5 4 3 2 1

Copyright Acknowledgments

Grateful acknowledgment is made to the following sources for permission to reprint previously published material:

Maria Montessori, *The Absorbent Mind* (Wheaton, Ill.: Theoretical Press, 1964), pp.
    67, 169, 246, 249, 261, 282; *The Montessori Method* (New York: Schocken Books,
    1964), pp. 61–62, 71, 84, 85, 87, 88, 92–93, 94, 109, 115, 228, 285, 287,
    304, 337, 348–49. Reprinted by permission of the publisher.
A. S. Neill, *Summerhill: A Radical Approach to Child Rearing* (New York: Hart Publish-
    ing Company, 1960), pp. 4, 35–36, 48, 107, 114, 118, 149, 155, 167, 195,
    250, 260, 284, 292, 294, 297, 348. Copyright © 1960 Hart Publishing Com-
    pany. Reprinted by permission of the publisher.
Jean Piaget, *The Construction of Reality in the Child* (New York: Basic Books, 1954), pp.
    231–32, 233, 258. Copyright © 1954 by Basic Books, Inc. Reprinted by per-
    mission of the publisher; *Play, Dreams and Imitation in Childhood* (London: Kegan
    Paul, 1951, and New York: W. W. Norton & Co., 1952), pp. 216–17, 224,
    225. Reprinted by permission of the publishers.

FOR

Anthea
Aleta
Amelie
Ariel
and
Sam

CONTENTS

ACKNOWLEDGMENTS

In this book I continue to try to work out a theory of education based on the philosophy of Sir Karl Popper. I thank him for his encouragement of my work. But he, of course, is not responsible for what I have done with his philosophy.

In preparing this book I have benefitted from numerous conversations with my friends and colleagues, Stephenie Edgerton, Christine Nystrom, and Neil Postman. I have received very helpful criticisms from Martin Hamburg and Gordon Pradl, who read an earlier draft of the manuscript. Most of all, I thank my students at New York University who have helped me learn from my mistakes.

Once again I am grateful to Marilyn Coppinger who typed, retyped, and retyped the manuscript with patience, intelligence, and goodwill.

The editorial staff of Greenwood Press has impressed me greatly by its professionalism, courtesy, and tact—supportive qualities rarely encountered today.

INTRODUCTION

It is difficult to be a teacher today.

Not because students—or parents, or school administrators, or classrooms—are different from what they used to be. No, it is difficult to be a teacher today because our present conceptions of education are *still* what they used to be. In conducting the various classes over which they preside, most teachers still adhere to a conception of education that dates back to the seventeenth century, a conception I call the transmission theory of education. They view education as a process like printing, wherein the teacher transmits or imposes knowledge into the minds of the students, just as the printing press imposes words on blank sheets of paper.

The transmission theory of education is both false and immoral. Education is not, nor could it ever be, a process of transmission. Moreover, when teachers try to convert education into a process of transmission they demean the humanity of their students and they themselves become authoritarian.

We are badly in need of a new conception of education. Actually, we have one at hand: the conception of education as growth. It is not new. Rousseau proposed it in the eighteenth century. But it remained a romantic, somewhat metaphysical conception of education until the

late nineteenth century, when John Dewey, under the influence of recent advances in the field of biology, developed a natural theory of
human growth. As I understand Dewey's theory of growth, however,
it is merely a new version of the old transmission theory. And when
teachers today do talk of education as growth, it is usually Dewey's
(transmission) theory that they have in mind.

In this book I argue that there is another theory of growth inherent
in the work of Maria Montessori, Jean Piaget, Carl Rogers, A. S. Neill,
and B. F. Skinner. I characterize it as a Darwinian theory, a theory
that says we learn from our mistakes. To make this argument, I have
to reinterpret the works of these theorists, recasting their ideas in ways
they never did and, perhaps, in ways they would oppose.

Why do it? Why not accept these theories as their creators presented them instead of interpreting (or reinterpreting) them? I think
that they must be interpreted or reinterpreted because all of these theories have given rise to successful educational practices.

And this creates a problem.

The Dewey Laboratory School worked, the Montessori method works,
Neill's Summerhill worked, Skinner's behavior modification works,
Rogers's student-centered pedagogy works, and the educational prac-
tices based on Piaget's theory about cognitive development also work.
By saying that these schools, these methods, these practices "work,"
I mean that the outcomes were as predicted by the theories the prac-
tices were based upon.

But all these successes lead us to question the adequacy of the different theories. Seemingly quite different from, even incompatible with,
one another, each theory—as originally presented by its creator—cannot explain the success of practices generated by the other theories.
Carl Rogers's theory cannot explain why behavior modification works,
nor can Skinner explain the success of child-centered pedagogy. Dewey
and Neill had very different theories of education, and both sharply
criticized the theories of Maria Montessori, whose success neither of
them could explain.

So, confronted with these very different yet successful educational
practices on the one hand and their corresponding, disparate, and
seemingly incompatible educational theories on the other hand, I
conclude that it must be the theories that are inadequate. We need
not abandon them, but we do need to reinterpret them.

In short, we do not need more empirical studies of the Montessori classroom. It works. What we do need are conceptual analyses that can explain *why* the Montessori classroom works. More than this, we need a theory that can, at the same time, explain why a Rogersian approach to education works, why Neill's Summerhill worked, why Skinner's operant conditioning works.

In fields outside of education, reinterpretation of the work of leading theorists goes on all the time. The best examples are in science, and the most famous instances are Copernicus, whose new theory reinterpreted the work of Ptolemy, and Einstein, who reinterpreted the work of Newton. We educators must begin to follow the path travelled in other fields.

It is time, I think, to abandon the antinomianism commmon in education today. "You like Dewey, she likes Rogers, I like Montessori," I hear teachers say. "We each have our own approach to education. No use arguing about which one is correct," they continue. "Whatever works for *you* is the best approach to use." Some teachers are eclectics. They pick and choose certain aspects of different theories that most appeal to them and then concoct their own "personal" theory of education, one that suits them or their style.

This all sounds nice and free and open, but making the choice of educational theory a matter of personal taste means that there can be no rational assessment of the worth of the various educational theories: "You like Dewey, she likes Rogers, he likes Skinner, just as you like Pepsi, she likes Coke, he likes root beer."

If eduational theories are simply a matter of personal taste, then we will choose them as we choose our drinks, our clothes, our home furnishings, our hairstyles. Some of us will be up to date, some of us will be old-fashioned. No one will be able to say that this is a better or worse theory than that one. There can be no progress, merely fads.

In other fields, one does not adopt a theory because it happens to please. One does not pick and choose between Einstein and Newton, or Copernicus and Ptolemy. One adopts Einstein's theory because it is superior to Newton's theory.

A more sophisticated version of antinomianism in education appears when educators say that Montessori, say, provides a good theory for some educational situations or some kinds of students, whereas Rogers, say, provides a good theory for other situations or other students. And the reason proffered for using Montessori in one situation and Rogers in another is that Montessori works in the first and Rogers works in the second.

But why? Why does Montessori or Rogers work in one situation and not in another?

To explain this we need a third theory, a metatheory—a theory that will accept the theories of Montessori and Rogers and explain both theories and their limitations. This is why Einstein's theory is superior to Newton's: it both accepts Newton's theory and reveals its limitations—and it explains both Newton's theory and its limitations.

My hope is that we can have progress in educational theory, and my suggestion is that we seek it by constructing new educational theories, or metatheories, that reinterpret those earlier theories that have generated successful educational practices.

In this book my thesis is that twentieth-century educational theorists have actually shared a hitherto unrecognized and unarticulated theory, or metatheory—a Darwinian theory that says "we learn from our mistakes." This theory contains a new conception of the student, a new conception of the role of the teacher, as well as a new conception of the content of education and a new conception of the aim of education.

PART I

Of Metaphors and Common Sense

1

THREE METAPHORS FOR EDUCATION

"A treatise on education," Emerson once wrote, "affects us with slight paralysis and a certain yawning of the jaws." Similarly a convention on education, a lecture, or a system. The very word "education," Emerson complained, has a "cold, hopeless sound."

Emerson was correct. Almost everyone will agree that education is a boring business, then and now. But why? Why are conversations about education so dreary? Books about it so dull? And educators themselves such uninteresting people? Is tedium inherent to this business?

Perhaps.

Yet another explanation is possible. I suggest that this reaction of weariness to the topic of education is actually a reaction to the metaphor we commonly use when we talk about it: the metaphor that construes education as a process of transmission.

This transmission metaphor was dominant in Emerson's time and still prevails in our own. According to this metaphor, education is a process, a process of transmission, not unlike the process of printing. Indeed, the metaphor came into vogue following the introduction of printing in the West. John Comenius (1592–1670), who might be called the father of modern educational theory, used the model of the printing press to explain how education took place.

"Instead of paper, we have pupils," Comenius wrote, "pupils whose minds have to be impressed with the symbols of knowledge. Instead of type, we have classbooks and the rest of the apparatus devised to facilitate the operation of teaching. The ink is replaced by the voice of the masters, since it is this that conveys information to the minds of the listener, while the press is school discipline, which keeps the pupils up to their work and compels them to learn."[1]

Comenius wrote this in the seventeenth century. Within two hundred years (by the time of Emerson, that is) this transmission metaphor for education had become a commonplace dominating all conventions on education, all lectures, all systems. It was this construction of education as a process of transmission that had given the word itself so cold, so hopeless a sound. Education had become a technique; its practitioners, technicians.

What is frequently not realized is that the transmission metaphor had replaced an older metaphor for education, a metaphor that today has all but disappeared from education discourse—nor does it exist in our present-day systems, lectures, and conventions.

This older metaphor had dominated all thought and talk about education for almost two thousand years, going back to the time of Plato. According to this older metaphor, education is not a mechanical process, like printing, but a human procedure, a procedure of initiation. Initiation into what? Here there were some disagreements about particulars, but there was a general consensus that education initiated students into a world beyond their present experience, a better world, a world where they could live a better life: a life of the mind.

Emerson's disaffection with education, I have suggested, reflected his animus toward the transmission metaphor of education. Yet this animus did not arise, on Emerson's part, out of any pining for the older metaphor of education as initiation. No, Emerson's opposition sprang from his advocacy of still a third metaphor, the newest, most recent metaphor: education as growth.

Education, according to this third metaphor, is development, the natural development of a person. Here, the teacher does not initiate students into the life of the mind, as the oldest metaphor would have it, nor does the teacher transmit knowledge and information to them, as the modern metaphor would have it. Instead, in accord with this latest metaphor, the teacher's task now is to create a proper environment, an environment that will promote "the growth of the individual."

Let me now sketch a brief history of these three metaphors and trace some of their consequences.

EDUCATION AS INITIATION

The most famous model of the initiation metaphor of education is Plato's myth of the cave. In the *Republic*, which he composed sometime during the first quarter of the fifth century B.C., Plato envisioned education as a long, arduous passage out of the darkness and the shadows of the nether world of the cave into the *real* world of truth and light. The cave represented the everyday world people experienced through their senses. But this everyday world is not, Plato insisted, the real world. Our sense observations do not grasp reality; they grasp only shadows or images of what is actually real. What is real are the ideas or forms that exist not in the physical world perceived by the senses but in another world, a world of spirit, a world of ideas. Only by passing out of the cave into the world of ideas—into the real world—can we grasp truth and understand the nature of things. We grasp truth only through our intellect, our developed intellect. And this is what education does: it develops the intellect, thereby initiating the student into the life of the mind.

So, for Plato, education is the procedure that initiates the young into the real world, the world of ideas, the world of truth and light, where they can live the life of the mind. The uneducated, those who remain in the cave—trapped in the world of physical appearances—can have only opinions, never true knowledge of the nature of things.

Plato's myth of the cave presents but one version of the metaphor of education as initiation. A second version, which historically was more pervasive in education, even during Plato's own lifetime, construed education as initiation of the young into their cultural tradition. Isocrates, a contemporary of Plato, was the first to construct this version of initiation, a version in sharp contrast to the philosophical, utopian scheme that Plato had put forth. Isocrates argued that even if there were a world of ideas, the journey to such a world would be long and the arrival uncertain. So Plato's model of a society where (some) people could live a life of the mind, contemplating true ideas and conducting the affairs of the society on the basis of their true understanding of the nature of things, simply could not work. This ideal of true knowledge was beyond the ken of human beings. Instead of striving for perfect truth, Isocrates counselled, men should guide their lives, and the affairs of society, by "right opinion."

When someone has right opinion, Isocrates explained, he does not possess truth or certainty about the nature of things. But when confronted with a problem to solve, or an issue to decide, the man with right opinion usually does come up with the best possible answer. The best possible answer is that one most in keeping with his cultural tradition. So men of right opinion come up with solutions that cohere with, or are intimated by, their cultural heritage.

Education, Isocrates concluded, consists of initiating the young into their cultural heritage. He would do this by having them study the written records of the best that had been said and done—the world of human achievement contained in the writings of the poets, the historians, the philosophers, and the statesmen of the past. This comprised their culture, what the Greeks called *paideia*. Those who had *paideia* had right opinion. When in the first century B.C., Cicero, the Roman orator and statesman, came to translate the term *paideia* into Latin, he called it *humanitas*. As a result, literature and history, and sometimes philosophy—those subjects that initiated the young into culture—came to be called the humanities. And the metaphor itself, the metaphor of education as a procedure of initiation, came to be identified as the humanist conception of education.

The study of the humanities supposedly helped one to become a human being. Indeed, humanists like Isocrates believed that people were not born human, they became human only through initiation into their culture. For Isocrates and for most Greeks (and later for the Romans, too), those who were not Greek (or Roman) were barbarians. And being Greek (or Roman) was a matter not of race or place of origin but of culture. "We call these people Greeks," Isocrates said, "who have the same culture we do, not the same blood."

The world of culture was not Plato's spiritual world of ideas, yet it too was a world beyond the ken of most people. It was a higher world, a world of sweetness and light, removed from the diurnal existence of most. It was reserved for those who could spend their youth at school, those who did not have to work to live—the *aristoi*. Note, too, that the school (*schola*), by definition, was a place set apart from the practical world, a place unrelated to the goings-on in that world. The school was the repository for the total cultural tradition, a tradition that at any particular time might be present in the real world in only an abbreviated version.

Yet although it was unrelated to the goings-on in the real world, getting an education was hard work. One had to study, and that called for industry, perseverance, precision, patience, and attention. The procedure centered on the subject matter, which consisted of books—not just any books, but classics, those that contained the best that had been said and done. Each student encountered these works and (with varying degrees of success) made the content his own: he acquired his heritage of understandings, feelings, imaginations, and beliefs—all that made him a cultured human being.

Because we are today so far removed from this construction of education, it is necessary to say a few words about what it means to become "cultured." One does not acquire culture as one acquires a suit of clothes nor in the way one acquires a suntan. This is not an exchange transaction or simply a matter of exposure. The acquisition of culture is a procedure of submission, simply because culture consists, in great part, of interdictions. We recognize a "cultured person" by that conduct he eschews, or will not perform. Yet for all its interdictory character, humanists view the acquisition of culture as a liberating procedure: a liberation from physical appetites and material desires. Equally important, education liberates one from the prison of the present. Initiation into one's culture thus constitutes a *liberal* education. Released from domination by his present appetites and desires, the student becomes less an animal and more a human being, capable of living the life of the mind. Education initiates one to the journey toward self-realization, toward the goal of becoming human.

A teacher is indispensable to this procedure of initiation. The teacher serves as the agent of civilization: someone who has mastery over one part of that cultural tradition, someone who can direct and guide the transactions between the student and the text, someone who can lead the student to willing submission to the interdictions of his culture.

The outcome of this humanist education is a cultured man who, freed from control by his appetites, liberated from the prison of the present, has become a good man, a gentle man—a member of the elite. A man so educated has an intellectual and moral identity; he is someone who has right opinion because he has achieved the condition of being human, a condition that is defined by his cultural heritage.

After flourishing in ancient Greece and Rome, this humanist construction of education lay dormant during the "dark ages" but came to life again as the "new learning" of the Renaissance of the fifteenth century. Combining the sacred texts of Christianity with the newly rediscovered secular texts of ancient Greece and Rome, Renaissance humanists revived and reconstructed education as a procedure of initiation into the Western cultural heritage, now redefined as the Greco-Roman Judeo-Christian heritage.

In the sixteenth century, the Protestant Reformation and the subsequent Catholic Counter-Reformation both initially splintered but then later solidified the emergent nation-states of Europe. These religious movements created an increased demand for education and educational facilities so that the people could preserve and pass on what had now become their version of the Western cultural tradition. So, in the sixteenth and seventeenth centuries, in every nation we find rulers creating, or encouraging the creation of, humanist schools: grammar schools in England, gymnasia in the German nations, and Jesuit colleges in the Catholic countries. Hand in hand with the erection of these new educational institutions, there appeared new introductory Latin grammar books that became quasi-official books for the educational institutions in each country.

In addition to the impact of religion on the educational arrangements during this period, there was the influence of politics. In every emerging nation of Europe during the sixteenth century, the rulers had need for administrators, judges, and governors to help manage the affairs of state. The humanist educators promised that the "new learning" would prepare the upper classes (and some lucky aspirants from the middling classes as well) to aid the rulers in performing these functions of government. A humanist education, they pointed out, developed "right opinion." Initiation into the cultural heritage brought about submission to the interdictions of that culture; it transformed boys into virtuous gentlemen, well prepared for, in the words of Thomas Elyot, "the distribution of justice in sundry parts of a huge multitude."[2]

By the seventeenth century, the "new learning" born in the Renaissance had come to dominate all thought and talk about education. The procedure for initiating the young into their cultural heritage consisted of studying, under a watchful teacher, the classical texts—both sacred and secular—of the past. And the schools set up to carry out this engagement harbored the future elite of each nation.

At this point, a new intellectual movement emerged that in time challenged, and ultimately overpowered, the humanist idea that education is a procedure of initiation. This movement, called the new philosophy, was originally neither a movement nor a philosophy but simply a concern among a few, a concern to better the quality of human life. When partnered by the belief that the means for bettering the quality of life had actually been discovered, this concern burst forth as the "new philosophy." In time, this new philosophy gave birth to a new metaphor for education: education as the transmission of knowledge.

EDUCATION AS TRANSMISSION

If we have to name names, then it is probably Francis Bacon (1561–1626) who is most responsible for the metaphor of education as transmission. It was Bacon's obsession with improving what he was fond of calling the human estate that led him to denigrate the study of the humanities along with the whole humanist conception of education. Books contain naught but words, he said, and words, Bacon sniffed, "are but the images of matter . . . to fall in love with them is all one as to fall in love with a picture." To improve our human estate, we must, Bacon insisted, pay heed to the nature of things themselves. We must study nature, not books. Direct experience, not reading, will reveal the secrets of nature. And understanding the nature of things— the scientific laws that underly all that happens—will enable us to improve the human estate.

Bacon, of course, was not without his religious sentiments. He believed that by knowing the true nature of things Christians could better appreciate the omniscience and omnipotence of the creator and so become more pious.

But the greatest error of all is the mistaking of the last end of knowledge. For men have entered into a desire of learning and knowledge, sometimes upon a natural curiosity and inquisitive appetite; Sometimes for ornament and reputation; and most times for lucre and profession; and seldom sincerely to give a true account of their gift of reason, to the benefit and use of man; as if there were sought in knowledge a shop for profit and sale, and not a rich storehouse for the glory of the Creator and the relief of man's estate.[3]

Although Bacon's immediate followers, like him, remained religious and viewed the advancement of knowledge as an activity that engendered Christian piety, the "new philosophy" did, nevertheless, in time undermine religious belief. For the "new philosophy" represented nothing less than the attempt to establish man's dominion over the universe. Bacon had put it tersely: "Knowledge is power." So, as he gradually advanced scientific knowledge (read: power), Western man increasingly had no need for a God to appeal to, nor for a faith to find solace in: now when the world oppressed him, Western man turned to science to improve his human estate.

Over the three hundred years following Bacon's death, the advancement of knowledge and the use of knowledge to improve the human condition led to a total reconstruction of the political, economic, and social arrangements of Western civilization. During this time, feudal political arrangements gave way to consciously designed constitutional governments. Over the same period, traditional economic arrangements disappeared as the agrarian-craft economy fell victim to the technological inventions that created industrial cities and made them the core of the economy. Social arrangements changed, too, as a "more rational" social order emerged when various groups— the clergy, the aristocracy, the landed gentry—were stripped of most of their social privileges and prerogatives.

In the very act of creating this modern, enlightened civilization to improve the human estate, the "new philosophy" destroyed the social controls that had been inherent in the traditional political, economic, and social arrangements. Industrialization, urbanization, secularization, nationalization—all products of this "new philosophy"—had all operated to free people from traditional constraints, thus creating a need for new forms of discipline and control. Ever optimistic about mankind's ability to improve the human estate, the advocates of the "new philosophy" had an "enlightened" solution to the problem of social control: education. In their hands, education took on a new construction, the role of the teacher changed, and there appeared new conceptions of the pupil and the content of education.

According to the "new philosophy," knowledge comes from experience. So children with their limited experience could not themselves "know" how they should behave. But adults, who have had more experience and who have reflected on the matter, will have such knowledge about how one should behave. And they can transmit this knowledge to the young—in the form of rules, or dictums, or better still, as John Locke suggested, in the form of habits. Children, Locke said, are like "balls of wax" that may be molded or shaped to the master's wishes. The "new philosophy" had announced that knowledge, true knowledge, was power. With true knowledge, man can control the world he lives in and thereby "improve" it; and with true knowledge he can also control, and also thereby "improve," his own behavior and the behavior of children.

What we have here is a new construction of education, a new metaphor. Education was no longer a procedure of initiation through which the young came to submit to the interdictions of their culture. Instead, education had become a process of transmission through which the young could be disciplined, or trained, or socialized to the wishes of the adults responsible for them. The hallmark of this new transmission metaphor of education was the belief that human beings learn from experience.

This new construction of education emerged from the epistemological optimism of Bacon and his followers, who believed that human beings could obtain true knowledge through sense experience, through sense observations. Plato, you will recall, had denied such epistemological optimism, insisting that sense experience resulted only in mere opinion. Bacon, however, and his followers in the "new philosophy" promised that one could arrive at true knowledge through sense experience *if* one followed the method of induction, the method of carefully observing a number of singular instances of some phenomenon and then inducing a general truth about it. (After carefully observing a great number of swans, for example, one could induce the general truth: All swans are white.)

This inductive method of arriving at truth created the idea of a "science" of education called instruction. Instruction is a technique, a technique for transmitting knowledge to pupils through their senses or sense experiences. By having students make repeated sense observations of the "material," the teacher "instructs" them. In time they "learn."

"The ground of instruction," wrote Comenius, "is that sensual objects may be rightly presented to the senses, for fear they may not be

received." But teachers up until that time *had not rightly presented objects to the senses*, he complained and so "the work of teaching and
learning goeth heavily onwards and affordeth little benefit."[4]

In order to present objects to the senses rightly, the matter to be
taught had to be broken up into simple components and then organized and sequenced—packaged. At this point, the classical texts students had studied in schools gave way to textbooks. Textbooks contained what pupils were supposed to learn, all set out in graduated order,
often illustrated with pictures and diagrams.

The substitution of textbooks for texts was but a small part of the
transformation in educational practices brought about by the new
transmission metaphor of education. The most salient changes were
in the roles of the teacher and the pupil. No longer a "master" who
initiated the young into their cultural heritage, the teacher now became an "instructor" who transmitted knowledge to a pupil. And the
pupil was no longer a "student" who studied the books that contained
that cultural heritage, for now the pupil became a "learner," someone
who more or less passively acquired knowledge through his own sense
experience.

Once the teacher had become an instructor, or transmitter, of
knowledge and the pupil had become a learner, then new questions
arose: What should the teacher transmit? What should the pupil learn?
What is worth knowing? With the older initiation metaphor of education, the matter of what was worth knowing had not been a problem. Then the student had studied (he did not "learn") his cultural
tradition in order to become a human being. But now, with the transmission metaphor, education was a matter of learning—learning from
experience. What, then, was he to learn?

Recall that the "new philosophy" had announced that it was possible for human beings to know the true nature of things. This, then,
is what pupils should learn: the true nature of the real world, including the physical world and the social world, too.

Such an education, like the traditional humanist education, liberated those who received it, although in a different way. Truth about
the nature of things makes people free by freeing them from ignorance
so that they can control their destinies and improve their conditions.
This belief in man's power to discover the truth released an optimistic
faith in man that contrasts starkly to the traditional humanist belief
in the authority of tradition. Tradition, said the humanist, would guide

man and save him from folly and wickedness. Not so, said the modern. Truth should guide man. And man can know the truth through experience and reason.

Yet in the very act of freeing man from the authority of tradition, the transmission theory of education lost what was liberating in the traditional education. Traditional humanist education, by initiating the young into their cultural heritage, intended thereby to free them from the prison of the present and from the domination of physical desires for material things. But modern education emerged out of the "new philosophy," which looked to the improvement of the human estate. To the new philosophers, knowledge was power, the power to control and shape. Modern education, therefore, embedded people more deeply in the present and enthralled them more completely to their physical desires for material things. Rather than liberate, modern education socialized the young—socialized them to the prevailing theories of the physical world, socialized them to existing social, economic, and political arrangements.

What helped to stamp modern education as an engagement to socialize the young was the fact that modern education initially emerged as an education designed for the lower classes. The lower classes had never been privy to the traditional humanist education. It was unthinkable that the lower classes should study the humanities in order to acquire the right opinion needed by leaders. No one had ever dreamed of liberating the lower classes to live the life of the mind. Not for them initiation into the cultural heritage.

But in the aftermath of the social, political, and economic upheavals caused by the religious wars of the sixteenth and seventeenth centuries, it became clear that the lower classes did need some looking after. They needed new constraints. They needed to become industrious workers, sober and stable members of the community, and subjects loyal to their rulers. They needed shaping and molding. They needed educative experiences to fit them to live in the existing world. They needed to be socialized.

From the seventeenth to the twentieth centuries, the transmission metaphor of education dominated all schools and school systems established to educate the masses. During this time the upper classes, however, continued to receive an education based on the metaphor of initiation. *Their* schools initiated *them* into the world of culture, preparing them for positions of leadership. But today all leaders must have expert knowledge about the nature of things—scientific knowledge about the real world, not knowledge provided by the humanities. As a result, the initiation metaphor that had long characterized the education of leaders has all but vanished in our time.

Today, the transmission metaphor dominates almost all educational institutions. Today, children of the upper classes as well as those of the lower classes are sent to school to be socialized, to learn those things that will prepare them to fit into the existing political, economic, and social arrangements. Today, all learn (or are supposed to learn) what is needed to be a productive worker, an active citizen, a cooperative member of the society. Today, almost all schools are places where teachers transmit (or are supposed to transmit) this knowledge to pupils. And today, all pupils learn this knowledge (or are supposed to learn it) through their own sense experiences.

Yet, although the transmission metaphor has come to dominate education in the Western world, it has not been without critics who have raised both logical and moral objections to it. The initial criticism of the transmission metaphor of education came in the eighteenth century, when David Hume (1711–76) demonstrated the logical impossibility of inductive learning from experience. He pointed out that no number of single experiences—whether of swans, oranges, triangles, or verbs—can allow us to infer a general truth about the objects observed or experienced. We can never logically induce any general truth about *all* oranges, *all* triangles, *all* verbs, *all* swans. No matter how many white swans we observe, we can never induce the general statement "All swans are white."

Yet even though Hume conclusively demonstrated that induction, or learning from repeated experiences, is logically impossible, he himself continued to believe that we do learn from experience. Induction, he suggested, must be a psychological rather than a logical matter. We do, he insisted, learn about a single instance through our sense experiences; thus, "This is a white swan, and that is a white swan, too." And although these and many similar experiences give us no *logical* basis for concluding that all swans are white, we have, Hume insisted, psychologial certainty that, indeed, all swans are white. This "psychological" interpretation of the process of induction "saved" the theory that we inductively learn from experience—saved it from the very criticism that Hume himself had levelled against it. Indeed, by now the belief that we inductively learn from experience has become part of the common sense of modern man.

So in spite of its logical inadequacies, the transmission metaphor persisted through the eighteenth, nineteenth, and into the twentieth century. It persists down to the present, where many educators still remain caught in its spell. Believing that we inductively learn from experience, they strive valiantly to *transmit* knowledge to their pupils. Inevitably, this leads teachers to authoritarianism: the attempt to secure greater control over the educational process. Take, for example, the subject matter: teachers who seek to transmit knowledge attempt to control the subject matter by packaging it into a transmittable curriculum—a spiral curriculum, or an experiential curriculum, or an activity curriculum, or a core curriculum, or an integrated curriculum, or some other package that will facilitate instruction. Take, as another example of authoritarianism, the treatment of pupils: teachers who seek to transmit knowledge to students attempt to control them; they "prepare" them, "stimulate" them, "motivate" them, "get them to pay attention," "get them moving." All these tactics are attempts to control pupils so that teachers can more expeditiously and efficaciously transmit knowledge. Thus, in abolishing the authoritarianism of tradition inherent in the initiation theory of education, the transmission theory merely substituted the authoritarianism of the teacher.

This inevitable authoritarianism of the transmission metaphor of education led Jean Jacques Rousseau (1712–78), a one-time close friend of David Hume, to criticize it on moral grounds. Here is his marvelous opening paragraph in *Emile*:

God makes all things good; man meddles with them and they become evil. He forces one soil to yield the products of another, one tree to bear another's fruit. He confuses and confounds time, place, and material conditions. He mutilates his dog, his horse, and his slaves. He destroys and defaces all things; he loves all that is deformed and monstrous; he will have nothing as nature made it, not even man himself, who must learn his paces like a saddle horse and be shaped to the master's tastes like the trees in his garden.[5]

Rousseau refused to construe education as a process of transmission. Education was not a mechanical process like printing, he insisted; it was an organic process like the growth of a flower: not a process of transmission, but a process of growth. Although educators might believe that they can transmit knowledge and thus produce an educated person, they cannot do this at all. Educators do not and cannot "produce" a learned person, he argued, any more than a gardener can produce a flower. A flower grows and develops naturally. The gardener does not produce it. He simply gives the young plant tender care and protection so that the flower will grow, naturally, spontaneously. When Rousseau looked at a child, he did not see a blank sheet of paper awaiting the imprinting of knowledge. No, what he saw was a living organism that, if properly tended and cared for, spontaneously develops or grows through natural stages of maturation.

As first introduced by Rousseau, the growth metaphor revolutionized the role of the teacher and the conception of the pupil. Education was to be child or pupil centered—not teacher centered or subject centered. And the teacher was no longer an instructor, or transmitter of knowledge; instead he became responsible for creating and maintaining an educative environment. For, you see, the pupil learned, or grew, naturally, without pushing, without pulling.

Unfortunately, Rousseau's construction of education as growth contained a totally inadequate conception of human growth. As he viewed it, human growth was a spontaneous unfolding of a human being's natural goodness, a process that occurred if the child were raised naturally—with no interference, no imposition of rules, no regulations, no habits. This was a metaphysical conception of human growth that rested upon faith rather than knowledge and called for pedagogical indulgence rather than pedagogical method.

It was not until the late nineteenth and early twentieth century that the American philosopher John Dewey (1859–1953) seemingly overcame the drawbacks by reconstructing the metaphor of education as growth. Under the influence of biological evolutionary theory, Dewey constructed a conception of educational growth that did eliminate the practical, romantic, and metaphysical liabilities of Rousseau's original version of the metaphor. But in the act of eliminating the difficulties created by Rousseau, Dewey created new difficulties for the conception of education as growth.

Although Dewey was born in the very year Darwin published his epochal *Origin of the Species*, it was not Darwin's theory of evolution that Dewey took up but that of his predecessor, Jean Lamarck (1744–1829). And in following Lamarck, Dewey converted the growth metaphor back into a version of the transmission theory of education.

According to Lamarck, evolution begins with a problem, a problem of adaptation to a changed environment. The occurrence of a problem signals a limitation, an inadequacy, or even a mistake inherent in

the organism or in its conduct. Because of this inadequacy, the organism cannot secure what it needs—food, water, air, or whatever is
necessary to survive. To solve the problem, the organism has to modify itself or its behavior. And then—and this is the central feature of
Lamarckism—the organism *transmits* these acquired characteristics to
its progeny. In this way, Lamarck explained, the species evolved, each
with its own specific characteristics.

Take the case of the giraffe with its striking characteristic of having
a long, long neck. How did such a creature evolve? Lamarck would
have us believe that in the far distant past the ancestors of the giraffe
grew long necks in order to reach the leaves on the topmost branches
of the trees. Then they transmitted long necks to their offspring. In
time, the story went, all giraffes had long necks.

In his educational theory, John Dewey was decidedly Lamarckian.
"Ability to make and retain a changed mode of adaptation in response
to a new condition," Dewey wrote, "is the source of that more exten-
sive development called organic evolution." This ability to make adaptations, this ability to solve problems, Dewey made the central feature of his theory of education. Education, he said, was growth; growth
was adaptation to changed environmental conditions. Organisms can
adapt or grow because they are what Lamarck took them to be: problem-solvers. Thus, children naturally learn, or acquire behavior
(adaptive behavior), when they are confronted by problems—just like
the giraffes who grew long necks when they had a problem.

By construing education as a process of growth through solving
problems, Dewey took Rousseau's metaphysical constructions of growth
as spontaneous unfolding and replaced it with a construction of growth
as a natural process. But in doing this he converted or reconverted
educational growth back into a process of transmission.

Following Lamarck, Deewey insisted that people acquire knowledge
through solving problems of adaptation. Therefore, he wanted teachers to present students with problems—real problems, meaningful
problems. But this was simply a better way for teachers to transmit
knowledge. For in solving the problems, pupils would acquire, or rediscover, that knowledge that adults already possessed; that is, they
would learn how people secure food, clothing, and shelter; how we
communicate messages, transport goods, and maintain our present social, political, and economic arrangements; how, in general, adults have
solved most human problems. Thus, Dewey's Lamarckism led him to

regard educational growth as a process of transmission—the transmission of acquired culture from adults to the young, not biological transmission, of course, but transmission by instruction.

What was original in Dewey's version of the transmission theory of education was that the process of instruction consisted of having the young *rediscover* the knowledge the adults already possessed, rediscover it by solving problems instead of having knowledge transmitted through set lessons.

Here Dewey assigned the teacher a role that is difficult to carry out. The teacher was to discover the correct "fit," the correct "match," between the student and the problem. The teacher was to know and understand each student's past, present, and future experiences, was to know the student's interests, his or her level of maturation. Possessed of this knowledge about the students, the teacher also had to have a broad, deep, and sophisticated knowledge and understanding of the subject matter to be taught. For the teacher's task was to fashion a problem for the students that would both engage them and promote their learning or growth.

Not unexpectedly, many teachers could not pull this off. Not all pupils learned what they were supposed to learn. The role assigned to the teacher was difficult, some said impossible, except for super-teachers.

Dewey admitted that this new conception of education as growth did give the teacher a difficult problem. But, he insisted, there was a method to solve that problem: the scientific method of experimentation. The teacher simply had to make experiments in order to discover, scientifically, the best solution to the problem of setting problems for students that would promote learning.

Dewey also said that the teachers should transmit this scientific method to their students. This experimental method, the method of science, was, he thought, the key to continual growth. It was the method of adaptation, the method for solving problems, the method for overcoming the limitations and inadequacies of our current knowledge or conduct.

What is important to realize is that Dewey viewed the scientific method as a way of getting answers, a way of solving problems—a way of adapting, a way of coming up with the best possible answers, the most correct solutions.

But Dewey was wrong about the scientific method. There is no method for adapting to the environment, no method for solving problems, no method for overcoming the limitations of our knowledge. Intelligence, thinking, the scientific method are not methods for coming up with answers or solutions. They are methods of testing or criticizing answers or solutions. No matter how carefully we think, how thoroughly we apply intelligence, or how dutifully we follow "the scientific method" to try to justify, prove, or establish an answer or a solution to a problem, no matter what we do, the answer will be inadequate, there will be something wrong with the solution. The most we can ever say about any answer is that so far it has survived all attempts to criticize it, to test it, to refute it.

Dewey greatly overestimated the ability of human beings to solve problems, to come up with correct answers. This overestimation of the intelligence of organisms and of their ability to control the future is inherent in the Lamarckian theory of evolution. Lamarckians assume that organisms consciously and deliberately solve problems and then consciously and deliberately transmit the solutions to their progeny. With Charles Darwin's theory of evolution, however, there is no such presumption of conscious intelligence. Evolution, according to Darwin, is a matter of luck, not cunning, a matter of blind trial-and-error elimination, a matter of natural selection. Darwinian evolution, or growth, is rooted in the ignorance and fallibility of organisms. Yet while most people today can accept this assumption of ignorance and fallibility in the realm of biological evolution, when it comes to the matter of the educational growth of human beings, many find it difficult to view this as a matter of trial-and-error elimination. The notion that educational growth takes place through trial-and-error elimination flies in the face of common sense.

It was John Dewey's adherence to the common sense theory of knowledge—or at least to parts of it—that led him to follow Lamarck and not Darwin in his reconstruction of the metaphor of education as growth. And this path, I have argued, reconverted educational growth into a process of transmission. During the twentieth century, other educational theorists have subscribed to the metaphor of education as growth. Like Dewey, these later theorists have had little influence on actual school practice, for most of what goes on in school today still remains under the spell of the earlier versions of the transmission metaphor. Yet the reason for these later theorists' lack of influence is quite different from the reason for Dewey's lack of influence. Dewey, I have argued, failed because, following Lamarck, he overestimated the intelligence of organisms. He assumed that, armed with the scientific method, human beings could solve problems and then transmit, via instruction, those solutions (and the scientific method, too) to the young. In contrast to Dewey, later twentieth-century educational theorists have followed Darwin. Their "Darwinism," however, like Dewey's "Lamarckism," was not conscious or deliberate. Hence, their Darwinism has gone unnoticed. Moreover, the very notion of a Darwinian theory of educational growth continues to fly in the face of a common sense theory of knowledge. I suggest, then, that the lack of influence of these later theorists on schools is due to the fact that teachers do not yet understand these theories, do not understand their Darwinian nature.

To pave the way for acceptance of my Darwinian interpretation of these later twentieth-century educational theorists, I must first try to undo the spell of this common sense theory of knowledge.

2

KARL POPPER'S EVOLUTIONARY EPISTEMOLOGY

THE COMMON SENSE THEORY OF KNOWLEDGE

The common sense theory of knowledge is made up of the traditional or "common sense" answers to four basic questions about knowledge: What is the nature of knowledge? Where does knowledge come from? How does knowledge grow? What is the basis or rationale for accepting knowledge?

With regard to the first question, about the nature of knowledge, the common sense theory holds that knowledge consists of ideas or concepts that are "in the mind." Plato seems to have invented this theory of the subjective nature of knowledge; or if he didn't invent it, he was the first to give it cogent expression.[1] Prior to Plato, people regarded knowledge as the quality of an act, or the mode or manner of performing, or the way of proceeding. All knowledge was knowing how: Achilles' knowledge of the arts of war, Hesiod's knowledge of the past, Aeschylus' knowledge of drama. All these examples of knowledge the Greeks regarded as instances of knowing how to act, how to perform, how to behave. With Plato, however, knowledge takes on a new guise. Knowledge, he said, consists of ideas or concepts: the "idea" of justice, the "idea" of a horse, the "idea" of the state, and so on. To know a horse, or the state, or justice is to have in the mind the correct "idea" or concept of each.

For Plato, knowledge of justice was no longer a matter of conduct; it now became a matter of grasping and possessing the idea of justice. Whereas prior to Plato to know a horse meant to be able to act in certain ways deemed appropriate vis-à-vis horses, now, Plato said, to know a horse meant to possess the "idea" of a horse.

Almost all philosophers since Plato have accepted his construction of the nature of knowledge, so it has become part of the common sense theory of knowledge. But most have rejected his answer to the second basic question.

The second basic question about knowledge is; Where does knowledge come from? (Or, if knowledge is ideas, where do ideas come from?) Plato had suggested that ideas are innate, that we are born with ideas that we can, through effort and training, recollect and grasp. His pupil, Aristotle, accepted Plato's notion that knowledge consisted of ideas in the mind but came up with a different explanation of the source of knowledge. We get our knowledge, or ideas, from the outside world, Aristotle said. Ideas come to our minds through experience. According to Aristotle, the mind is like a bucket, empty at birth, but into which ideas enter through the senses. The bucket theory of the mind is perhaps the most pronounced feature of the common sense theory of knowledge.

To the third question—How does knowledge grow?—the answer invented by Aristotle, and later made central to the modern version of the common sense theory by Francis Bacon, is that knowledge grows through induction. That is, the accumulation of ideas from experiences allows us to draw inferences or make generalizations. Observing a number of white swans, for example, allows us to draw the inference that all swans are white. All swans are white is a universal concept or idea that grew or evolved in our mind through inductive inference. We infer a universal concept or idea (all swans are white) from a number of singular ideas or concepts (this is a white swan; this is another white swan; this is still another, and so forth).

The final aspect of the common sense theory of knowledge has to do with rationality. According to the common sense theory, to be rational means to accept only ideas or concepts that are true. True ideas are those that can be demonstrated to be so, ideas that can be justified. This theory of rationality goes back to Plato, who originally made the significant distinction between knowledge and opinion. Unless we can justify a concept or an idea, then, Plato said, it is merely opinion, not knowledge. It is not rational to accept opinion as knowledge.

The Spell of the Common Sense Theory

These traditional answers to questions about the nature, source, growth, and acceptability of knowledge—all of which go to make up what I have called the common sense theory of knowledge—is probably the theory of knowledge most people presently subscribe to. I suggest that adherence to this theory of knowledge predisposes them to accept the transmission metaphor of education and the Lamarckian theory of cultural evolution. For what we have here are theories about knowledge, education, and growth that are not only related to one another but deeply embedded in each other. Acceptance of the Lamarckian theory of growth presumes acceptance of the transmission theory of education, which, in turn, presumes acceptance of the common sense theory of knowledge. Or, conversely, acceptance of the common sense theory of knowledge predisposes people to accept the transmission theory of knowledge, which, in turn, predisposes them to accept the Lamarckian theory of cultural evolution.

If, as I have claimed, twentieth-century educational theory is based on a Darwinian theory of education and growth, then adherence to a Lamarckian theory of growth will be a barrier to understanding twentieth-century educational theory. But because the Lamarckian theory has its root in the common sense theory of knowledge, it is necessary to attack directly that common sense theory of knowledge, to try to dislodge it and replace it with an alternate theory. Only in this way can we hope to break the spell that prevents us from understanding and effectively using twentieth-century educational theory.

The work of Sir Karl Popper contains the most sustained attack on the common sense theory of knowledge in the history of philosophy. Moreover, Popper has produced an alternative theory of knowledge to replace what he has refuted. Popper's repudiation of the common sense theory of knowledge came about as a result of his lifelong study of the growth of scientific knowledge, which, he found, takes place through Darwinian selection: scientific knowledge evolves through the critical elimination of theories that are unfit. This discovery led him to challenge the Lamarckian theory of cultural evolution and to argue that the evolution of culture, like the evolution of the species, is better explained by Darwin's theory. In the course of constructing his theory of the Darwinian growth of scientific knowledge, Popper has confronted the common sense theory of knowledge in all its aspects.[2] In what follows, I will use his arguments and present his own theory of Darwinian evolutionary epistemology to try to break the spell of the common sense theory of knowledge.

FALSIFIABILITY: A NEW CRITERION FOR SCIENTIFIC KNOWLEDGE

Karl Popper's earliest interests in the philosophy of science centered on the problem of demarcating science and nonscience. How can one distinguish scientific knowledge from nonscientific knowledge? What about Marxist theories? Freudian theories?

The most dominant influence on his life, Popper tells us in his autobiography, was Albert Einstein. The successful test of Einstein's theory in 1919, when Popper was seventeen years old, gave the world a new cosmology—a real improvement on the cosmology of Newton. Yet it was not so much the success that impressed Popper as it was Einstein's own clear statement that he would regard his theory as untenable if it should fail certain tests. This critical approach to theory was, Popper concluded, the true scientific attitude. Instead of looking for verification of theories, one looked for crucial tests that could refute the theory tested, although they could never establish it.

This notion of refutation provided Popper with the criterion to demarcate science from nonscience. "If somebody proposed a scientific theory he should answer, as Einstein did, 'Under what conditions would I admit that my theory is untenable? In other words, what conceivable facts would I accept as refutations or falsifications, of my theory?' "[3] In his *Logic der Forschung* (1934) Popper introduced the idea of falsifiability (or testability, or refutability) of a theory as a criterion of demarcation.

To many people, then as now, Popper's criterion for the demarcation of science makes no sense. It violates common sense—the common sense theory of knowledge. Falsification and falsifiability cannot tell us what theories to accept, these critics insist, it cannot tell us which theories are true, it provides no rational basis for science at all.

This objection to Popper's proposed criterion springs, of course, from the justificatory theory of rationality, which is itself part of what I have called the common sense theory of knowledge.

Actually, this theory of justificatory rationality has, since the time of Bacon, served as the criterion for demarcating science from non-science: Science consists of those theories that have been justified or confirmed by experiment. Thus, to establish the superiority of his proposal to use falsifiability as the criterion for demarcation, Popper had to refute the justificatory theory of rationality and replace it with a new theory.

Critical Rationality

In opposition to the justificatory theory of rationality, Popper has argued that we can never justify a theory. To do so is logically impossible, and all such attempts lead to an infinite regress. For we can always challenge any so-called justification by asking for *its* justification. And since no claim is justified unless *its* justification is also justified, then justification is simply logically impossible. And if justification is impossible, then rationality, as defined, is impossible.

A. This claim c is true.

B. How do you know c is true?

A. Because c follows from d, and d is true.

B. How do you know d is true?

A. Because d follows from e, and e is true.

B. How do you know e is true?

A. Because e follows from f, and f is true.

B. How do you know f is true?

A. Because . . .

One way to avoid the infinite regress is to accept some final authority that itself has no need of justification (for example, sense experience, intuition, self-evidence, or some other final authority).

B. How do you know f is true?

A. Because I can see f with my own eyes (or because f is self-evident).

B. How do you know that what you see with your own eyes is true?

A. Because sense observation is the authority for truth.

But to appeal to some final authority (sense observation, for example) is to abandon rationality as defined. For now, one winds up accepting a claim—that all sense observations are true—that is not itself justified or confirmed. So, once again, we see that justificatory rationality is logically impossible.

To replace the logically invalid common sense theory of justificatory rationality, Popper has put forth his theory of critical rationality. According to critical rationality, we should give up looking for justification for knowledge and instead look for errors, inadequacies, and limitations that inhere in our present knowledge or follow from it.

What then does it mean to be rational? According to Popper, it is rational to accept (or prefer) *tentatively* those theories, or statements, or propositions, or conducts, which have stood up to criticism. We might even say that we are "justified" (in a different sense of the word) in preferring a theory that has stood up to criticism better than its competitors.

Note that Popper's critical rationality is not tied to a quest for certainty. It is the quest for certainty that has led most people to equate knowledge with demonstrable truth and, therefore, rationality with justification. The critical rationalist, however, is not trying to establish the truth of a statement, so critical rationality escapes the logical pitfalls of justificatory rationality. For the critical rationalist, there is no point at which one can stop criticizing a theory and conclude that the theory is true. Criticism can continue indefinitely. All one can ever say of a well-criticized theory that has withstood all tests is, "So far, it has not been falsified; therefore, I will prefer it to other theories that have not withstood these tests."

Because it avoids the logical difficulties of justificatory rationality, critical rationality is clearly the better theory of rationality. And so we can now understand why falsification is a better criterion than justification for demarcating science from nonscience. For although we can criticize scientific statements, we can never justify them, justification being logically impossible. And we accept (tentatively) those statements that our criticisms have not, so far, actually falsified. Here we can see how Popper's theory of critical rationality underlies his proposal to use falsification as the criterion for demarcation: we can only criticize statements that are, in fact, capable of being falsified; hence, nonfalsifiable statements are not science.

Yet in spite of its logical superiority, many people have trouble accepting Popper's theory of rationality and so still cannot accept falsifiability as the criterion for demarcating science from nonscience. This resistance comes, in part, from their subscription to yet another part of the common sense theory of knowledge: the common sense theory about the nature of knowledge.

Objective Knowledge

According to the common sense theory, knowledge consists of ideas or concepts in the mind. So, if all knowledge is subjective, then how can anyone be critical of knowledge? We can criticize the "knowledge claims" of someone else, the argument goes, but we do this on the basis of our own subjective knowledge. We can never actually criticize our own knowledge.

The trouble with this common sense theory about the nature of knowledge is that if all knowledge is subjective, then we cannot account for scientific knowledge. For if all knowledge is subjective, then we cannot say of any two theories about the same phenomena that one theory is better than the other—we can only believe one and doubt the other. But belief, even strong belief, does not allow us to demarcate science from nonscience. Thus, if all knowledge is solely subjective, then the ideas of physics are simply the ideas that physicists believe to be true. But this gives us no way to demarcate physics from astrology, since astrology is also a matter of belief. Who can say that the beliefs of the physicists are better than those of the astrologers? Indeed, if knowledge is simply a matter of belief, then there is no way to distinguish sense from nonsense. The lunatic who believes he is a coconut can be condemned only on the grounds that his is a minority belief. In sum, the theory that all knowledge is subjective makes rationality impossible.

In contrast to the common sense theory about the nature of knowledge, Popper has proposed a theory of objective knowledge. He has suggested that we may distinguish the following three worlds or universes (without, be it noted, taking the words "world" or "universe" too seriously): first, the world of physical objects or of physical states; second, the world of states of consciousness or mental states, or perhaps, of behavioral dispositions to act; and third, the world of objective contents of thoughts, consisting of problems, theories, and arguments as such. World two contains subjective knowledge. World three is the world of objective knowledge.

One of the most startling conjectures that Popper makes about the inmates of world three—theories, problems, arguments, for example—is that these are not merely expressions of subjective mental states. These entities, he says, exist independently of world two. They exist outside our minds. Knowledge in this objective sense is totally independent of anybody's claim to know; it is also independent of belief or disposition to assent, to assert, or to act. "Knowledge in the objective sense is knowledge without a knower; it is knowledge without a knowing subject."[4]

One example that Popper uses to demonstrate the independent existence of world three inmates is arithmetic:

A number system *may* be said to be the construction or invention of men rather than their discovery. But the difference between even and odd numbers, or divisible and prime numbers, is a discovery: these characteristic sets of numbers are there, objectively, once the number system exists, as the (unintended) consequences of constructing the system, and their properties may be discovered.[5]

The situation is similar with regard to scientific theories. Every scientific theory has, objectively, a huge set of important consequences, whether or not they have yet been discovered. The objective task of the scientist—a world three task—is to discover the relevant logical consequences of the new theory and to discuss them in the light of existing theories.

These considerations do establish the existence of an objective and autonomous world three—a world of theories, of problems, of arguments. Yet many people have difficulty in accepting the theory of objective knowledge that underlies Popper's theory of critical rationality, which in turn underlies his proposal to use falsification as the criterion of demarcation. How can human beings obtain objective knowledge? they ask, for according to the common sense theory, knowledge comes to us through experience, through our sense observations. How then can human beings obtain objective knowledge through sense experience? Popper has called this the bucket theory of the mind and has rejected it as a totally inadequate explanation of the origin of knowledge.

Conjectural Knowledge

Doubts arise about the bucket theory of the mind when we recall the case of Helen Keller, who, although blind and deaf, did attain a remarkable degree of intellectual development. Although he has frequently brought up the case of Helen Keller, Popper's main argument against the bucket theory of mind is a logical one. He maintains that it is logically impossible for knowledge to originate in sense observation.

In a number of lectures and articles, Popper has demonstrated this by challenging people: "Observe!" When told to observe, most people respond by asking, "What do you want me to observe?"

Observations, Popper argues, come *after* expectations. It is logically impossible to observe without a problem or question—an expectation. So one must begin with expectations, not observations. If expectations *must* logically precede observation, then, Popper concludes, there must be inborn expectations. The newborn infant cannot simply observe; it must have been born with expectations. Popper, of course, does not accept the notion of inborn ideas, which, he says, is absurd, but every organism has inborn reactions or responses, which he calls dispositions, expectations, or even theories—without implying that they are conscious.

The newborn baby has theories about the world and its relation to itself. It has a disposition to try to suck everything that comes into, or near, its mouth. It expects to be nourished. It has a theory about the relation between the world and itself: the world is for sucking.

Some of these theories (dispositions, expectations) are actually built into the sense organs. Take the primitive sense organs of the lowly paramecium. When it collides with an obstacle, the paramecium reverses its movements and swims forward in another direction. Built into the sense organs of this creature is the mechanism to react in this way. The paramecium is born with the disposition to back up and then swim forward in another direction when it bumps into an impenetrable something. Moreover, it is born with the theory that the object that gives it a jolt will remain at that point; otherwise a change of course might bring it into collision with the same obstacle.[6]

One of the most important inborn expectations, Popper says, is the expectation of finding regularity. Organisms have an inborn propensity to look for regularities. As Ernest Gombrich has put it, we have an inborn sense of order. The expectations of order must logically come before any observation, Popper argues, for all observation involves the recognition of similarities, or dissimilarities. But similarities or dissimilarities can only mean similarity for us, or dissimilarity for us. It is *we* who respond to situations as if they were equivalent or not, *we* who take them as similar or not, *we* who interpret them as repetitions or not. Therefore, we must have an inborn expectation of regularities.

Here Popper cites an experiment where a lighted cigarette was held near the noses of a couple of young puppies. After sniffing it once, they turned tail and refused to come back to the source of the smell to sniff again, and a few days later they reacted to the mere sight of a cigarette, or even of a rolled up piece of white paper, by bounding away and sneezing. As Popper interprets this occurrence—one of a kind common enough to all who have had young animals about—the puppies' conduct showed that they interpreted the second situation as a repetition of the first, that they expected its main element, the objectionable smell, to be present. The situation was a repetition—for them—because they responded to it by anticipating its similarity to the previous one.[7]

The totality of expectations an organism has at any moment makes up what Popper calls its horizon of expectations. The horizon of expectations plays the part of a frame of reference, a cognitive map.[8] But our maps, or our theories—including those we are born with—are not reliable; our expectations are often disappointed. Disappointed expectations constitute a problem for the organism.

When confronted with a problem, a disappointed expectation, we, like all organisms, come up with trial solutions—new conjectures, new hypotheses. These new trial solutions come about as modifications, or changes, in the theories, or the dispositions, or the conduct that has proved unreliable. Recall the conduct of the paramecium: it continually modifies its behavior in the light of disappointed expectations, moving backward and then off again in a new direction with every jolt. So with the baby trying to put something into its mouth: it continually modifies its conduct in light of its disappointed expectations. So with the mechanic trying to repair an engine, or an artist painting a picture—they continually modify their conduct in light of disappointed expectations. And so with a scientist trying to explain some going on in the universe, or a historian recreating something that happened in the past—they continually modify their theories in light of disappointed expectations.

In summary, Popper has argued that sense observations cannot be the source of knowledge since, logically, theories must precede observation: we need to have expectations before we can observe. Moreover, he points out, "theories," or dispositions to react or to respond, are built into our physical makeup: we are born with theories. In time, he says, we modify and change these theories, dispositions, expectations when they prove unreliable. From this he concludes that knowledge comes from us: knowledge is conjectural. We create it; we are the source of knowledge.

It is important to note that Popper's conception of conjectural knowledge includes the knowledge created by the paramecium as well as what we call scientific knowledge. There is no difference between the paramecium and the scientist with regard to the source or origin of knowledge. Science, Popper has written, is a "straightforward continuation of the pre-scientific repair work on our horizons of expectations."[9] Like the paramecium, the scientist never starts from scratch. At every instance, science presupposes a horizon of expectations, a collection of tentative theories, which, when their inadequacies are discovered, will be repaired or modified.

Although all organisms create knowledge, only humans can create objective knowledge, and humans alone can be rational (that is, critical). And this is possible because of human language. In a number of places, Popper has discussed what he calls the functions of language. First, there are what he identifies as the two lower functions of language: self-expression and signalling. In the self-expressive function, language is symptomatic of the state of some organisms—for example, cries of fear, pain. In the signalling function, language releases or elicits a response from another organism—warnings, pleas, and so on. All animal languages and all human languages share these two lower functions. But human language has many other functions, the most important of which are the descriptive function and the argumentative function.

With the development of a descriptive language, a linguistic world three can emerge, and with it the regulative idea of truth emerges, that is, of a description that fits the facts.

The fourth function of human languages, the argumentative function, presupposes the descriptive function: arguments are fundamentally about descriptions; they criticize descriptions from the point of view of the regulative idea of truth. Thus, the development of the descriptive function of language is a necessary precondition for the existence of objective knowledge (world three); and the development of the argumentative function is a necessary precondition for criticism (critical rationalism.) The descriptive language creates the *object* for our critical discussion. And, with the evolution of the argumentative function of language, criticism becomes the main instrument of the further growth of knowledge.[10]

Here we can pause to point out some of the connections among Popper's answers to the problem of knowledge. As to the matter of the origin or source of knowledge, Popper has put forth the theory that organisms create knowledge. In creating knowledge, the scientist is no different from the paramecium. But the nature of the knowledge that the scientist creates is different from the knowledge the paramecium creates. Popper has put forth the theory that the scientist creates objective knowledge. Because he can encode his theories in descriptive language, the scientist can create a linguistic world three, a world of objective knowledge. It is only when knowledge becomes objective that criticism—or what Popper has called critical rationality—is possible. The paramecium cannot be critical vis-à-vis its expectations, or theories, because it cannot *face* them: they are part of it. Subjective knowledge becomes criticizable only when it becomes objective, and it becomes objective only when we *say* what we think and, even more so, when we write it down or print it.[11]

Popper's theory of conjectural knowledge underlies his theory of critical rationality and helps to explain why people have trouble accepting his theory of critical rationality. For if someone is under the spell of the common sense theory of knowledge, he believes that the source of knowledge is external to the knower. He believes the human receives his knowledge through sense observation, and then the question of its acceptability becomes a matter of justifying it. But if knowledge is, as Popper suggests, conjectural, then it can never be justified; it always remains conjectural. And the only way we can ascertain its acceptability is via criticism: we accept that knowledge (those conjectures) that has withstood our efforts to criticize it. And the only way we can demarcate scientific knowledge from nonscientific knowledge is through the criterion of falsifiability. Scientific knowledge (conjectures about the real world) is capable of being falsified, capable of being refuted.

Yet many people still have difficulty accepting the theory that all knowledge is conjectural, that all knowledge comes from us. They cannot give up the notion that we receive our knowledge from the external world. To deny this, they argue, is to deny that we learn from experience. Here, we encounter the fourth aspect of the common sense theory, its theory of how knowledge grows. According to the common sense theory, knowledge grows through induction. Through repeated experiences we come to know something, or to know how to do something. Thus, repeated observations of white swans lead us to induce the knowledge that all swans are white. In the same way, repeated practice on a typewriter leads us to knowledge of how to type.

Conjectures and Refutations

Popper's argument against induction, like all of his arguments against the other aspects of the common sense theory, is a logical one. Earlier we saw that he argued against justificatory rationality by pointing out that it led to an infinite regress, while he argued against observation as the source of knowledge by showing that it was logically impossible. His logical arguments against induction follow those first made by David Hume. Hume argued that we cannot logically reason from "instances of which we have experiences to other instances of which we have no experience." We cannot, for example, reason from a number of observed white swans to the conclusion that all swans are white. Although we have experienced "instances" of white swans, we cannot reason that all those we have not experienced are also white. Someone might try to argue, however, that in cases like white swans we can rely on past experiences: if we have experienced a certain number of instances of constant relationships, then we have also experienced that those relationships continue to hold in yet unobserved cases. But here, too, the response is the same. As Hume put it: "I would renew my question *'why from this experience can we form any conclusion beyond those past instances of which we have had experience?'* "

A_1 From my observation of x number of white swans, I conclude that all swans are white.

B_1 But how can you reason from what you have experienced to what you have not experienced?

A_2 From my past experience I know that when I observe a certain constant relationship between objects in x number of instances, that this constant relationship will hold in all cases.

B$_2$ But how can you reason from what you have experienced to what you have not experienced?

A$_3$ From my past experiences I know that when I observe such relationships as experienced in A$_2$, in x number of instances then such relationships have held in all cases.

B$_3$ But how can you reason from what you have experienced to what you have not experienced?

A$_4$ From my past experience . . .

Hume's argument shows that any attempt to justify the practice of induction by an appeal to experience must lead to an infinite regress. Popper accepts Hume's argument as a conclusive logical refutation of induction. He does, however, prefer to reformulate it in objective (world three) terms, rather than in the subjective, psychological (world two) languages Hume used. Here's how Popper prefers to state the question: Can we reason from singular statements (Hume's instances of which we have had experience) to the truth of universal statements (Hume's instance of which we have had no experience)?[12]

Popper, agreeing with Hume, says no: no number of true observation statements can justify the claim that a universal theory is true. Thus, the logical problem of induction is solved—negatively. Induction is logically impossible.

Yet people *do* expect and *do* believe that instances of which they have no experience will conform to those of which they have had experiences. People do believe, for example, that the sun will rise tomorrow.

Hume thought that people did do this. So in spite of the fact that induction is logically impossible, Hume insisted that people do reason inductively. And people do it, Hume thought, because of conditioning or habit. He believed that our knowledge is conditioned by repetition. So if we do observe a number of white swans, for example, we become conditioned to expect that all swans are white—even though there is no logical basis for concluding this.

Popper has argued against Hume's contention that people are conditioned by repetition to believe that instances of which they have no experience will conform to those of which they have experience. It is, he says, logically impossible to acquire beliefs through repetition. Here, Popper uses the same infinite regress argument that Hume himself had used to explode the logical theory of induction. Repetition, he reminds us, presupposes similarity, and similarity presupposes a point of view—a theory, or an expectation. A repeated observation, say, of a white swan, presupposes that the observer perceives the second observed swan as similar to the first, and to do this, the observer must have an expectation, a theory, about the two observations that make the first observation similar to the second. In other words, the theory "all swans are white" could not have been the result of conditioning, the outcome of repeated observations of white swans, since in order to experience a repetition, one must already have a theory that all swans are white.[13] Here is how Popper puts it:

Similarity-for-us is the product of a response invoking interpretations (which may be inadequate) and anticipations or expectations (which may never be fulfilled). It is, therefore, impossible to explain anticipations, or expectations, as resulting from many repetitions as suggested by Hume. For even the first repetition-for-us must be based upon similarity-for-us, and, therefore, upon expectations—precisely the kind of thing we wished to explain.[14]

Hume's explanation that induction is a matter of conditioning, Popper concludes, involves him in an infinite regress. Therefore, induction does not exist. Neither animals nor men use any procedure like induction. The belief that we use induction is simply a mistake. It is a kind of optical illusion.[15]

If knowledge cannot grow through induction because induction does not exist, then how does knowledge grow? Popper's answer is that knowledge grows through conjecture and refutation, through the procedure of trial-and-error elimination. Recall, first of all, Popper's contention that all knowledge is conjectural. This means that the growth of knowledge consists of replacing our conjectures with better ones.

How do we do this?

Knowledge originates, we saw above, with a theory—and in the first instance with inborn theories in the form of dispositions and expectations. But then our experiences, our observations, reveal that some of our theories are false. This creates a problem for us: our problems arise when one or more of our theories have run into difficulties. Because we have a sense of order, an expectation of regularities, we try to solve the problem by creating a new conjecture, to modify, change, refine the theory that has proved to be inadequate. But in time we find out that the main conjecture solves the problem only in part, or that it creates new problems. This, in turn, prompts us to create new conjectures, new theories.

   This is how knowledge grows. We begin with theories that give rise to problems, which prompt us to make new conjectures, new theories, better theories, which, in time, give rise to new problems, which prompt us to make new conjectures, new theories. . . . And so it goes. Each new theory is better than its predecessor insofar as it does not have the same inadequacies, the same limitations, the same errors, as the one it replaces. Each new theory, however, will have its own limitations and errors—as yet undiscovered. Our theories, Popper says, are like trial balloons. When we discover and eliminate the errors they contain, we improve them. The growth of knowledge is a procedure of trial-and-error elimination.

   This procedure of trial-and-error elimination looks like induction, but its logical structure is totally different. With induction, the purported logical structure is that of reasoning from instances of which we have experience to the truth of corresponding laws or to instances of which we have no experience. This, we saw, is logically impossible, nor can it be a matter of conditioning either. But it is logically possible to reason from a counter-instance to the *falsity* of the corresponding universal law (any law of which it is a counter-instance). "This is a black swan" is a counter-instance to the law"all swans are white." Acceptance of one counter-instance to "all swans are white" implies the falsity of the law "all swans are white." The logical structure here is deductive:

1. If all swans are white, then it follows that this swan will be white;
2. But, this swan is not white;
3. Therefore, it is false that all swans are white.

   In deductive logic, the falsity of the conclusion is retransmitted to (at least) one of the premises. This is how refutations are made. As Popper puts it, "Induction is logically invalid, but refutation is a logically valid way of arguing from a single counter-instance to—or rather, against—the corresponding law."[16] Thus, although the growth of knowledge looks like a process of inducing general laws from particular instances, this is not what is going on at all. For the growth of knowledge is a procedure of conjecture and refutations, a matter of trial-and-error elimination: we make conjectures and then modify or replace them when we discover counter-instances. And the logical situation used in this procedure is deductive logic.

Since knowledge grows through the discovery of counter-instances, or contradictions, then the great instrument for the growth of knowledge is criticism. It is through criticism that we can, if we are lucky, discover counter-instances, or contradictions, to our theories and thus reveal their limitations and inadequacies. So if we want to contribute to the growth of knowledge, we must, Popper says, adopt a critical approach toward knowledge.

Popper insists that it is criticism, the tradition of criticism, that is the hallmark of science. What makes the scientist different from the nonscientist is the conscious and deliberate adoption of a critical approach toward all knowledge. This is why the history of science is a history of the advancement or the growth of knowledge.

Contrast, once again, the paramecium and the scientist. Both the scientist and the paramecium, we saw, create their knowledge. And both advance their knowledge via trial-and-error elimination, although the scientist has an advantage insofar as he can encode his knowledge in world three language and thus more readily detect its errors. But now Popper is bringing out another important difference between the scientist and the paramecium, a difference in their attitudes toward error.

The scientist, unlike the paramecium, consciously tries his best, whenever a solution occurs to him, to fault it and detect an error in it: he approaches his solution critically. By adopting a consciously critical approach toward knowledge, the scientist can eliminate inadequate solutions, which then leads to the creation of better solutions, in other words, to the growth of knowledge: the replacement of inadequate conjectures with better ones.

One last point on the paramecium and the scientist. Both of them can and do err; both make mistakes. Even though the scientist employs the critical approach to eliminate erroneous theories, he can only eliminate a finite number of theories and can never reduce the infinity of surviving possible theories. As Popper puts it: "Einstein may err, precisely as the amoeba may err." What this means is that we can never attribute truth or probability to our theories. We can only say of a theory that it is false, or a better theory, than one of its predecessors.

At this point, we reach the heart of Popper's conception of human beings: human beings are fallible creators of knowledge. We have seen that all knowledge is conjectural, which means that we cannot justify it. But we can improve our conjectures by subjecting them to criticism. This possibility of *continued* improvement follows directly from our being fallible creators: since knowledge can *never* be perfect, then it can *always* be improved.

From this conception of human beings as fallible creators, it also follows that we should look on ourselves (and all organisms) as problem-solving rather than end-pursuing.[17] For, since our conjectures will always be limited, inadequate, mistaken, or false, then it follows that our conjectures will always generate new problems. So we are continuously and continually engaged in problem solving. And the problems we are trying to solve are generated by those earlier conjectures, or theories, which we created to solve earlier problems. Another way of putting this is to say that human beings continuously engage in the pursuit of truth. They do this in a backward and negative fashion— by eliminating the errors and mistakes in the knowledge they have already created.

Popper does not deny that we learn from experiences, but he has recast the role that experience plays in the growth of knowledge. Growth consists of the modification or refinement of existing knowledge. But we modify existing knowledge *only* when we discover that it is wrong. Therefore, growth depends upon experiencing mistakes, errors, inadequacies; growth comes out of negative experiences, the experience of disappointed expectations. As long as we experience no counter-examples to our conjectured theories, experience no disappointed expectations, we do not change our theories: our knowledge remains unchanged; it does not grow.

I have tried to show how Popper's solution to the problem of demarcation of science from nonscience has led to the creation of a totally new epistemology, an epistemology that refutes and replaces the traditional common sense theory of knowledge.

To review, Popper's epistemology gives us completely new answers to the four basic questions about knowledge:

1. *What is the basis or rationale for accepting knowledge?* Popper's criterion of falsifiability that he used to demarcate science from nonscience gives rise to a new theory of critical rationality: the acceptability of a statement depends upon how well it has withstood criticism.

2. *What is the nature of knowledge?* The theory of critical rationality

gives rise to the theory of objective knowledge. Knowledge can be criticized because it has an independent existence. It is part of what Popper calls world three. Knowledge can and does exist without a knowing subject.

3. *Where does knowledge come from?* The theory of objective knowledge rests upon the theory that all knowledge is conjectural. We do not receive knowledge; we create it. Knowledge comes from us.

4. *How does knowledge grow?* The theory that all knowledge is conjectural leads to the theory that knowledge grows through a procedure of conjecture and refutation, through trial-and-error elimination.

Evolutionary Epistemology

In recent years, Popper has characterized his theory of knowledge as a Darwinian theory and given it the name "evolutionary epistemology." According to Darwin's theory, the species evolved or grew as the result of chance mutations followed by the selection or elimination of the unfit. So also with knowledge: our knowledge consists at every moment of those conjectures that have shown their (comparative) fitness by surviving so far in the struggle for existence, a competitive struggle that eliminates those conjectures that are unfit. All selection is error elimination, and what survives—after elimination—as "selected," are merely those trials that have not been eliminated *so far.*[18]

Viewed in this light, the growth of knowledge is a matter of adaptation to the environment, adaptation through selection and trial-and-error elimination. This view encompasses animal behavior and prescientific knowledge as well as scientific knowledge. "From the amoeba to Einstein," Popper has written, "the growth of knowledge is always the same: we try to solve our problems, and to attain, by a process of elimination, something approaching adequacy in our tentative solutions."[19]

Animals, even plants, are problem-solvers. And they too solve their problems by the method of trial-and-error elimination. The tentative solutions they come up with to their problems are incorporated in their behavior or in their organs. These are, Popper says, biological analogues of theories. Like theories, they are conjectural, tentative adaptations to the world. These conjectures, whether in the form of theories, or behavior, or organs, do exert influence on the world (world

one), creating new ecological niches for organisms, which then lead
to the emergence of new problems. These new problems stimulate new
creations, new evolutions, new growth.

Popper has described this Darwinian theory of growth by the following schema:

$$P_1 \; \rightarrow \; TT \; \rightarrow \; EE \; \rightarrow \; P_2$$

We start from some problem, P_1, proceed to a tentative solution or
tentative theory, TT, which may be (partly or wholly) mistaken. In
any case, it will be subject to error elimination, EE, which may consist of critical discussion or experimental tests. Then new problems,
P_2, arise from our creative activity, and these new problems are not
in general intentionally created by us but emerge autonomously from
the field of new relationships, which we cannot help bringing into existence with every action, however little we intend to do so.[20]

TWENTIETH-CENTURY EDUCATIONAL THEORY: LEARNING FROM OUR MISTAKES

Earlier I argued that the traditional transmission theory of education assumes acceptance of the common sense theory of knowledge.
According to this common sense theory, knowledge is subjective, it
exists only in the mind of the knowers, we receive it from outside of
our selves, its acceptability depends upon how well it can be justified,
and, finally, it grows via induction. I have shown how Karl Popper
has criticized and totally destroyed this common sense theory of
knowledge. He has shown that induction does not exist, that it is logically impossible to receive knowledge from outside ourselves, that it
is logically impossible to justify knowledge. And he has argued that if
knowledge were solely subjective, then rationality would be impossible, there would be no way to distinguish science from nonscience,
sense from nonsense.

We can conclude, therefore, that like the theory of knowledge on
which it is based, the transmission theory of education is false. Teachers do not transmit knowledge to students. And they do not do this
because it is impossible for such a thing ever to happen.

Karl Popper has done more than destroy the transmission theory of
education. He has also given us a new theory of knowledge, a Dar-

winian theory of evolutionary epistemology upon which it is possible to build a new theory of education—a Darwinian theory of education. This theory of education can perhaps be called learning from our mistakes. Its most salient features are a new conception of the learner and a new conception of the role of the teacher.

According to this theory, the learner is active, not passive; a creator, not a receptor, of knowledge; a seeker of order, not needing motivation or control in order to learn. The learner learns from making mistakes.

As to the role of the teacher, this Popper-Darwinian theory rejects the notion that a teacher is a transmitter-controller and replaces it with a notion of the teacher as someone who creates an educative environment, an environment in which the student can learn from his mistakes.

In the chapters that follow, I want to show how this new theory of education is inherent in the works of the leading educational theorists of the twentieth century. None of these theorists has consciously formulated his or her educational theories on the basis of Popper's Darwinian theory of knowledge. But by interpreting each of these educational theories in light of Popper's theory of knowledge, I hope to begin to create a comprehensive synthesis of twentieth-century educational theory.

PART II

How We Learn from Our Mistakes

3

JEAN PIAGET

The common sense theory of knowledge has it that we receive our knowledge. We learn from our experience. So most people, if they have had the same kind of experiences, all share more or less the same understandings about the world.

The work of Jean Piaget (1896–1980) refutes this common sense theory about the source of knowledge. Piaget discovered that children understand the world differently from adults. More importantly, he found out that children have the same kind of mistaken understandings of the world at certain clearly demarcated ages.

Young children of four or five years of age, he found, for example, understand that a tall, thin glass contains more water than a short, fat glass, even though they see the water poured from one glass into the other. Piaget says that children this age do not yet possess the concept of conservation, according to which objects, or quantities, remain constant—are "conserved"—in spite of changes in appearance. Lacking this concept of conservation, children of this age think that the tall, thin glass contains more water. Not until they reach six or seven years of age do children understand that the amount of water in both glasses is the same.

In another experiment conducted with infants, Piaget discovered that until they reach about one year of age, babies "lose interest" in objects when they are out of sight. When his daughter, Jacqueline, was an infant, he tells us, she was fascinated by his pocket watch. But he found that she lost interest in this, or in any object, when he covered it with a blanket. Then, at about eight months of age, she began to reach under the blanket for the "vanished" watch. The child, Piaget says, had begun to develop the concept of "object permanence": objects "out of sight" were no longer "out of mind."

How can we explain why children understand the world differently from adults? More importantly, why do all children continue to make the same mistakes until they get older? It's not that children's minds function differently from adults: Piaget has shown that all children—even the very youngest—classify and relate phenomena; they have theories of causality, time, space, number, and the like. But they perform these functions differently from adults. What is different about children, Piaget says, is the structures of their minds. They do not have the same cognitive structures that adults have. These structures develop over time, which means that all children go through stages of cognitive development.

Since we construct our understandings of the world by means of these cognitive structures, this means that children will have understandings of phenomena that are different from the understandings that adults have of those same phenomena.

THE FOUR PERIODS OF COGNITIVE DEVELOPMENT

Piaget has identified four periods of cognitive development: 1. the sensory-motor period (which lasts for the first two years of life); 2. the preoperational period (lasts from two to seven years of age); 3. the concrete operational period (from seven to eleven years); 4. the formal operation period (eleven years to adulthood).[1]

During each of these periods, children develop the ability to perform certain kinds of actions. In marking off these periods, Piaget directs our attention to the limited kinds of activities children can perform at each stage of development. Thus, in the sensory-motor stage, children can only perform sensory-motor actions: they can look, listen, touch, smell, taste, cry, and make other noises; they can move their limbs, their fingers, and so on. Over the first two years of life, they exercise and elaborate these abilities so that they can grasp objects, push them, throw them, put them in their mouths, or in boxes; they develop a whole repertoire of noises and sounds; they become proficient at creeping, crawling, walking, and running.

In the next period, which Piaget calls the preoperational period, children can talk. Although Piaget does not distinguish the different functions of language, we can here follow Popper and note that during this preoperational stage children develop the ability to make sounds: 1. to signal; 2. to express their feelings and demands; 3. to describe; and 4. to argue, although not logically. At the same time, of course, they continue to exercise and improve their sensory-motor skills.

In the third period, the concrete operational period, children can perform logical operations with concrete objects. They can understand the relationships that exist among various objects: "this blue pencil is longer than that red one, so the red one is shorter than the blue one"; "all ducks are birds, but not all birds are ducks." They can figure out and explain how lots of things work. They can make and test predictions about the behavior of concrete objects: "this piece of wood will float, but this piece of metal will sink." They can follow and understand arguments about concrete objects.

In the last period of development, which Piaget calls the formal operational period, children can perform logical operations on propositions: "If Socrates is a man and all men are mortal, then Socrates is mortal." They can understand the formal logical relationships among propositions: "if p, then q; p, therefore q." They can draw implications from propositions and recognize contradictions between propositions.

There is nothing strange or unusual about this periodization. People have long known that children do not begin to talk until around two years of age and cannot think very well much before the age of seven. Piaget has merely elaborated and described more fully these periods of development.[2] But Piaget has done more than simply classify periods of development. He has put forth a theory about how this development takes place.

THE CONSTRUCTIONIST THEORY OF KNOWLEDGE

Piaget's genius lies in taking these long-recognized facts about what children can and cannot do and making them the basis for a constructionist theory of knowledge. According to Piaget, human beings construct knowledge. We do not receive knowledge, we create it. We are not passive receptors, we are active creators. And we create knowledge through the actions we perform—sensory-motor acts, language acts, and logical acts. Since infants can perform only sensory-motor operations, they create knowledge or understandings quite different from what adults can create.

Piaget's analysis of the procedures human beings go through in creating knowledge are somewhat murky, but the general outline is clear. The actions that people perform (sensory-motor actions, language acts, and logical operations) create or invent theories (or schemes and concepts, as Piaget calls them). People then use these theories (or schemes and concepts) in constructing their understandings of the situations they encounter.[3]

This constructionist theory of knowledge explains why infants understand the world differently from adults. Infants can perform neither language acts nor logical operations; therefore, they can create only sensory-motor or perceptual schemes, or how-to theories, about the world. Having limited theories with which to construct their understandings of the situations they encounter, infants have a limited understanding of all things. The same analysis applies to preoperational children, who, although they can perform language acts and so can create better concepts, or theories, about the world than sensory-motor children, still have limited understandings because they cannot perform logical operations.

Look at the water-in-the-glass experiment again. One way of interpreting this is to talk about the concept, or theory, of identity that preoperational children have. Children at this preoperational stage always mistakenly say that the amount of water in each glass is different because, according to the theory of identity shared by children of this age, the amount *cannot* be identical. Preoperational children have a theory of identity based solely on sense perceptions. One might call it a theory of complete perceptual identity that goes something like this: for *this* to be the same as *that*, it must look (or taste, or feel, or sound, or smell) the same. With this theory of identity, preoperational children construct their understandings of the situations they encounter: the amount of water in *this* tall, thin glass is *not* the same as the amount of water in *that* short, fat, glass, because the water level in this tall, thin glass is higher.[4]

All preoperational children share this perceptual theory of complete identity, and they use it to construct their understandings, to make sense of the situations they encounter. This explains why young children often get confused and even frightened the first time they see their grandmother wearing a hat. They perceive *this* (new) person in the hat as someone different from *that* (old) person whom they call grandmother. According to their perceptual theory of identity, *this* person is different from *that* person because this person looks or appears different. Similarly, children often fail to recognize a close relative, like their grandmother, if she is lying in bed, or wearing new eyeglasses, or if she laughs loudly—if, in short, she appears different in any way. Here is an example of the perceptual theory of identity from one of Piaget's observations of his daughter, Jacqueline, when she was two years and seven months of age (2:7).

Seeing Lucienne (her sister) in a new bathing suit with cap, Jacqueline asked:

"What's the baby's name?" Her mother explained that it was a bathing costume, but Jacqueline pointed to Lucienne herself and said: "*But, what's the name of that?*" (indicating Lucienne's face) and repeated the question several times. But as soon as Lucienne had her dress on again, Jacqueline explained very seriously: "*It's Lucienne again,*" as if her sister had changed her identity in changing her clothes.[5]

In addition to a theory of identity, children create other basic theories that they use to make sense of things, theories about space, about time, about causality, about chance, about reality. Piaget has carefully studied the development of these theories.[6] During the first two stages of development (the sensory-motor stage and the preoperational stage), these theories are all based upon sense perception. That is, children create these theories through their sensory-motor activities: by tasting, touching, and pushing things, by looking at things, smelling them, and listening to them.

Take causality, for example. Piaget has identified two different kinds of theories that sensory-motor children initially create about causality and then use to make sense of the situations that they encounter. According to the initial theory, which he calls the efficacy theory of causality, sensory-motor children theorize that external happenings are caused by one's self, or one's actions. Here is Piaget's observation of his son, Laurent, at the age of three months, twelve days (0:3 (12)):

Several days after he revealed his capacity to grasp objects seen, Laurent is confronted by a rattle hanging from his bassinet top; a watch chain hangs from the rattle. From the point of view of the relationship between the chain and the rattle, the result of the experiment is wholly negative: Laurent does not pull the chain by himself and when I place it in his hands and he happens to shake it and hears the noise, he waves his hand, but drops the chain. On the other hand, he seems immediately to establish a connection between the movements of his hand and those of the rattle, for having shaken his hand by chance and heard the sound of the rattle, he waves his empty hand again, while looking at the rattle, and even waves it harder and harder (he has already executed behavior of this type during the preceding days).

Observing that the rattle no longer moves—and this is what we wanted to come to—or rather, no longer seeing anything of interest in it, Laurent looks again at his hands, which he is still waving. He then examines most attentively his right hand, which he is swinging, meanwhile retaining exactly the same facial expression he had when watching the rattle. It is as though he were studying his own power over it. (Just as he has already seen his power over the rattle.)[7]

The second kind of causal theory Piaget discovered was that sensory-motor children create what he called a phenomenal theory. With the creation of this theory, the child ceases to consider his own actions as the sole source of causality and now attributes causal powers to someone else, or to someone else's body. According to this causal theory, contiguity causes change; that is, temporal and sometimes spatial contiguity between two events means that one causes the other. Piaget observed this theory emerge in his son Laurent during his eighth month (0:8):

With respect to Laurent, this new form of causality appears at 0:8 (7) in the following circumstances. I tap my cheek with my left middle finger, then drum on my eyeglasses (he laughs). Afterward, I place my left hand halfway between his eyes and my face, but without blocking his view. He looks at my glasses, he grasps my hand, and pushes it toward my face. Again I drum on my glasses and then put my hand in the previous position; he pushes it back more decisively each time. Finally I remain motionless; he grasps my hand and with it, hits, not my face, which he cannot reach, but the top of my chest.

A month later, I lower my hand very slowly, starting very high up and directing toward his feet, finally tickling him for a moment. He bursts out laughing. When I stop midway, he grasps my hand or arm and pushes it toward his feet.

At 0:9 (0) he grasps my hand and places it against his belly, which I have just tickled. He thus merely sets my hand in motion and does not strike it as before as though my activity depended entirely on him.

At 0:9 (6) similarly, when he is in bed he directs my hand to the bars to urge me to scratch them as I was doing before.

At 0:9 (13) Laurent is in his baby swing, which I shake three or four times by pulling a cord; he grasps my hand and presses it against the cord.[8]

When children enter the preoperational period and begin to speak, these efficacy and phenomenal theories of causation find expression in what Piaget calls egocentric and animistic theories of causality. He has collected many delightful examples of these kinds of theories from his painstaking observation of preoperational children. Here are some observations of his daughter, Jacqueline:

At 4:6 (2) she was afraid when she saw me going off on a friend's motorcycle. She put her fingers to her mouth in a special way, which was new, and said to her mother: "I'm putting my fingers like that so that daddy'll come back." At the same period, she stamped her foot in her room, saying: "I'm stamping because if I don't the soup isn't good enough. If I do, the soup's good." Obviously, nothing in these behaviors could have been suggested by the adults with whom Jacqueline lived. For instance, neither her parents nor her nurse were accustomed to stamp their feet.

When Jacqueline was 5:6 (11) I overheard a conversation between her and Lucienne in bed. Lucienne was afraid of the dark and Jacqueline was reassuring her. Lucienne then asked: "Where does the dark come from?" "From water, because when it's daylight, the night goes into the lake." But at 5:6 (22) I heard Jacqueline alone in the garden saying: "I'm making the daylight come up; I'm making it come up (making a gesture of raising something from the ground). "Now I'm making it go away (gesture of pushing something away) and now the night's coming. I make the night come up when I go to the edge of the lake"; "the man (walking outside the garden) still has a bit on his coat"; "I'm making the light come up." After this, she amused herself the rest of the day in "making light" with a stick (making the gesture of pulling it towards her and throwing it away).[9]

Here are some examples of the animistic theory of causality that preoperational children use to make sense of the situations they encounter. With this theory, children construct understandings that impute motives to inanimate objects.

Child (8:6): "The moon looks at us and watches over us. When I walk, it walks; when I stand, it stands still. It copies me like a parrot."
Adult: "Why?"
Child: "It wants to do whatever I do."
Adult: "Why?"
Child: "Because it's inquisitive."

Adult: "Why are there waves in the lake?"
Child (6:0): "Because they've been put there."[10]

In addition to egocentric and animistic theories of causality, preoperational children sometimes merely juxtapose or associate perceptions to explain causality.

Adult: "Why does the sun not fall down?"
Child (6:0): "Because it is hot. The sun stays there."
Adult: "How?"
Child: "Because it is yellow."[11]

Adult: "What makes the engine go?"
Child (4:0): "The smoke."
Adult: "What smoke?"
Child: "The smoke in the funnel."[12]

Later, when children reach the operational stage, they can create logical theories and use them to construct much improved understandings of the situations they encounter. These new theories they create about reality, time, space, causality, and identity now have a logical coherence. Here is an example of an operational child using a logical theory of causality to construct his understanding of a steam engine: "(At 8:0): 'There is a big fire. The fire makes a bit of iron go that's sort of bent (connecting rods), and that makes the wheel turn.' "[13]

As a final example of the theories about causality that children have at different ages, we have the following answers that Piaget got to the question: What makes the clouds move along?

(At 7:0): "It's the sun . . . with its rays. It pushes the clouds."

(At 8:0): "When we run along, they run along too."

(At 8:7): "It's the air which they (the clouds) make, and then it (the air) chases the clouds."

(At 9:6): "Because of the wind. They move along by the wind."[14]

Piaget's analysis of the different understandings that children have at different ages reveals that human beings do construct their knowledge. No one ever told a child that the sun does not fall down because it is yellow, or that somebody put the waves in the lake. Moreover, although children do construct their own individual understandings—one child thinks the sun pushes the clouds, another thinks the clouds run along when we do, another thinks the wind chases them—all these understandings have a filial similarity which indicates that each child employed the same kind of theory, an animistic theory, to construct them. And acording to Piaget, children of the same age have the same kinds of theories—about causality, say, or identity, or space—because they create these theories through the actions that they can perform, and the kinds of actions children can perform (sensory-motor, linguistic, logical actions) emerge over time in an invariant sequence.

As creators of our knowledge, however, we human beings are obviously fallible. The theories we create and the understandings we construct with those theories are often inadequate, false, mistaken. And nowhere is this more evident than with the knowledge that young children create. Yet, as Piaget's work demonstrates, much of the knowledge that children create does, in time, improve. Gradually they eliminate, or overcome, their false theories, their mistaken or limited understandings. In time they come to share the theories and the understandings of most adults.

How does this happen? It happens, I suggest, because children, like all of us, learn from mistakes.

Notice that Piaget's discovery of the cognitive differences between children and adults demonstrates that children *always* have mistaken understandings of the world, mistaken or inadequate understandings that they, in time, overcome or eliminate. Mistakes, then, seem to be a necessary part of learning: we learn from them. Piaget never said we learn from mistakes, but his theory of cognitive development can be interpreted that way.

LEARNING FROM OUR MISTAKES

We have seen that children have understandings of the world different from those of adults. This is because children, like all of us, construct their understandings by means of their theories, or concepts and schemes. These theories, in turn, are the product of human actions—sensory-motion actions, language acts, and logical operations. Children under two years of age can perform only sensory-motor actions and, therefore, have theories and understandings different from (not so adequate as) the theories and understandings of children two years and older, who can perform language acts, while children seven years of age or older can perform logical operations and so can create even better theories and thus construct better understandings.

This procedure of constructing our understandings is what Piaget calls the cognitive function of assimilation. He has taken the term "assimilation" from the realm of biology, where, as we know, organisms use their physiological structures to assimilate nutrients from the environment. Piaget argues that this is what happens in the cognitive realm. Human actions, Piaget says, have structures. Hence, there are sensory-motor structures, language structures, and logical structures. He calls all of these cognitive structures. Human beings use their cognitive structures to assimilate knowledge from the environment. In the biological realm, the physiological structures act on the environment and transform it into nutrients; in the cognitive realm, cognitive structures act on the environment and transform it into knowledge.

It is important to note that in cognitive assimilation, the organism does not ingest, or "take in," or "absorb" the environment, or any part of the environment. The environment simply presents the organism with something to be understood. Understanding is a process of construction. We use our theories to construct our knowledge, or, as Piaget puts it, we assimilate the world to those theories (schemes and concepts) we have. In this way, we *make* sense of the world. Knowledge is created, not received.[15]

Since very young children cannot perform language acts or logical operations, the knowledge or understanding that they can construct (assimilate) is limited by their sensory-motor cognitive structures. Yet we know that children do, in time, develop the ability to perform language acts and then, later, logical operations. How can we account for this development?

Piaget explains this by identifying a second cognitive function, which he calls accommodation. Accommodation, as Piaget views it, takes place when human beings modify or reconstruct the structures and the theories through which they create knowledge. Here, too, as in the case of the other cognitive function of assimilation, Piaget finds a parallel in the realm of biology, where organisms do modify their physiological structures in order to accommodate to the environment. Piaget's favorite example is the pond snail, *Limnaea*, found in the great Swiss lakes. He discovered that when these snails are exposed to continual intense wave action they produce a novel physiological structure that enables them to accommodate to the changed environment and thus survive.[16]

Piaget finds the same function of accommodation in the cognitive realm: human beings change or modify their cognitive structures and their theories which they use to create (assimilate) knowledge. Accommodation is possible, Piaget points out, because the cognitive structures have common structural elements. That is, although sensory-motor actions, language acts, and logical operations are all different kinds of human actions, they nevertheless have the common structural elements of certain order relations, subordination schemes, and correspondences.

We can readily see that these structural elements are present in the structures of language acts and logical operations: logical operations, like explaining the second law of thermodynamics, consist of ordering, subordinating, and establishing correspondences among objects and terms and propositions. With language acts, like describing a game of baseball, we employ the same structural elements—ordering, subordinating, and establishing correspondence—but here with words rather than propositions. Piaget also finds these same elements in the structures of our sensory-motor actions. Thus, there are order relations in reflex acts, in habitual acts, and in acts when we suit means to end. So when a sensory-motor child—an infant—pulls something, it is using the scheme (or "how-to" theory) of *grasping* and subordinating it to the more complex scheme ("how-to" theory) of *pulling*. As for correspondence, Piaget finds that infants are able to recognize and classify objects. The infant, of course, does not have the ability to use language to say, "That is my rattle," but the infant does shake its legs, or its hands, or may even jump and wiggle when it encounters the rattle. The infant's behavior manifests this "correspondence" activity whenever it is unexpectedly confronted by a familiar object—an object that the infant recognizes and classifies.[17]

Since the structures of the sensory-motor actions have the same elements as the structures of both the language acts, which develop later, and the logical operations, which emerge still later, then, Piaget argues, the structure of language acts and the structure of logical operations both have their roots in the earlier structures of the sensory-motor actions. The language acts are modifications or reconstructions of the earlier sensory-motor actions, and the logical operations are, in turn, reconstructions of the language acts. This procedure of modification of existing structures is what Piaget calls accommodation.

(Although Piaget does not explicitly do so, I think it is helpful here to distinguish between two kinds of accommodations: structure accommodations and theory accommodations. In structure accommodations human beings modify or reconstruct their cognitive structures. In theory accommodations it is the theories [or the schemes and concepts] that are modified.)

How does accommodation take place?

The notion of equilibration provides the key for Piaget. He defines equilibration as "an active compensation set up by the subject against exterior disturbances, whether experienced or anticipated."[18] Equilibration is a process of autoregulation that Piaget sees at work in the biological realm as well as in the cognitive realm. In the biological realm, the pond snail, *Limnaea*, that accommodated to the waves in great Swiss lakes is an example of biological equilibration: an active compensation against exterior disturbances.[19]

In the same way, Piaget argues, we have equilibration in the realm of cognitive development. That is, when the cognitive structures of young children cannot assimilate (create) adequate or correct knowledge, then children, in time, accommodate by creating new structures by modifying the old. This restores the equilibrium between the organism and environment, enabling it now to assimilate (create) adequate knowledge.

Why do organisms equilibrate? Piaget answers by claiming that all manifestations of life give evidence of the existence of organization. In both the biological realm and the cognitive realm, organisms organize, or seek order. In the cognitive realm, human beings seek coherence in their understandings of the world. They try to make sense of the situations they encounter, the experiences they have. So when human beings experience cognitive disequilibrium, a cognitive conflict—when they cannot make sense of what is going on, when they come up with inadequate or incorrect understandings—they try to restore equilibrium, overcome the incoherence, establish order.

According to Piaget, the quest for order is inherent in human beings. We try to establish cognitive order at whatever level of development we may be. That is, children at the sensory-motor level, for example, when they experience cognitive disequilibrium because they cannot make sense of a situation they encounter, try to restore equilibrium by employing their existing schemes and theories—or perhaps even creating new ones—to construct a better understanding of the situation. They cry out, they shake and strike out, they bounce, wiggle, and jump, they bite, scratch, and hold their breath, and so on. If it is an object, they touch it, and so on. Later, children at the preoperational period likewise employ the concepts or theories they have to restore equilibrium when they cannot make sense of a situation they encounter. They ask many questions: "What's that?" "Is it an animal?" "Is it a dog?" "Why?"

One way of putting all this is to say that we modify our structures and/or our theories when we discover that they have led us to construct incorrect, inadequate, limited, or mistaken understandings of a situation: we learn—and develop—by making mistakes. The discovery of a mistake leads us to modify our theories (and during the stages of cognitive development, to modify our cognitive structures) because we seek order—cognitive order, or coherence. To put it negatively: human beings seek to avoid mistakes.

We recognize a mistaken understanding when we confront a contradiction to that understanding, a counter-example. This contradiction may take the form of an unanticipated perception, an unexpected happening, an unacceptable proposition, statement, or claim, anything, in short, that refutes our understanding of a situation. Although we, because we seek coherence, always try to overcome the contradiction, we do not always discard our present understanding and try to construct a different one that is better. We are not always so ready to admit we are wrong in our present understanding. We sometimes simply deny or ignore that proposition, or that happening, or that perception that contradicts our present understanding. We become dogmatic.

Another way of overcoming the contradiction, however, is not to ignore it but to try to construct a new understanding, a better under-standing, one that avoids this recognized contradiction. This results in learning, or, if such an understanding involves changes in cognitive structures, it results in cognitive development.

Recall the experiment Piaget performed with his pocket watch. Up until she was eight months of age, his daughter Jacqueline "lost interest" in the watch when Piaget covered it with a blanket. For her, the watch had ceased to exist. This is because she, like all infants, had a perceptual theory of existence that went something like this: that only exists which I see. According to *this* theory, objects out of sight do not exist. And so, Piaget's infant daughter "lost interest" in objects when they were out of sight.

All infants have this theory, or scheme, of existence, of reality. The fact that this theory means that nothing then has permanent existence does not frighten or confuse infants (probably because whatever the infant has need of—its mother, or its mother's breast—always come into existence when the baby needs it, or when the baby cries). At any rate, having things pop in and out of existence seems to delight infants, as witness the universal appeal of the game of peek-a-boo, where adults vanish and reappear over and over again.

In addition to the sensory power of sight, the infant uses the senses of touch, hearing, taste, and smell to create theories about existence, or reality. Initially, as Piaget has shown, the infant uses each of these senses to create a different reality, or space field (oral fields, visual fields, tactile fields, and so forth). Not until about eight months of age does the child coordinate these fields into a general theory of reality, or existence.[20]

Prior to its eighth month, then, the child has a theory that goes something like this: that only exists which I can see, *and* that only exists which I can hear, *and* that only exists which I can touch, *and* that only exists which I can taste, *and* that only exists which I can smell. When the child does coordinate these different spatial field theories into one general theory of existence, it will go something like this: that only exists which I perceive.

This new, integrated theory is an improvement over the earlier un-coordinated perceptual theories of existence the infant had created. But this new theory is inadequate, too; indeed, it is false. So when the child uses this theory to construct her understanding of the situations she encounters, she comes up with contradictions.

As long as the infant does not recognize the contradictions inherent in her theory of existence, she then continues to lose interest in objects hidden from view, continues to accept that those objects do not exist even though they do continually reappear, or regain existence. She "sees" no contradictions. Finally, however, the contradictions force themselves on her, or she becomes conscious of them. The child comes to recognize these contradictions because she assimilates different (contradictory) sense perceptions. Recall the experiment with the watch under the blanket: I do not see the watch, so it no longer exists. But I hear the watch, so it does exist. Once the contradictions become manifest, once the infant recognizes and accepts the presence of a contradiction, she tries to overcome it by modifying the old theory in order to eliminate the inadequacies she now recognizes inhere in it. This results in a new theory, a theory the child has created, a new theory that makes better sense of the world, a theory that enables her to construct better understandings of goings-on. This better theory goes something like this: that exists which is *capable* of being perceived. As the child develops this new theory over time, she begins to look for balls and other objects that "vanish" under the blanket, objects that make no noise and are no longer visually perceptible but that the child "knows" do exist because she now has a theory that "tells" her that the object could not have vanished—it is simply hidden from view.

Let me now summarize how Piaget's work explains how we learn from our mistakes. Piaget has traced human cognitive development to our efforts to maintain cognitive equilibrium, which is to say, to our inherent quest for order. Cognitive disequilibrium consists of recognized contradictions to our understandings of the situations we encounter. Since we construct our understandings by means of theories, then that appearance of a contradiction indicates that one or more of these theories may be inadequate or false. (It may be, of course, and often is, simply a *mis*understanding which then creates an *apparent* contradiction. We clear this up with new or additional information.)

According to my interpretation, Piaget's single most important contribution to the educational theory that we learn from our mistakes is his conception of the learner: human beings are active creators of knowledge who seek order. This stands in marked contrast to the conception of the learner inherent in the transmission theory of education, which held that human beings are passive receptors of knowledge who require motivation and control.

According to my interpretation of Piaget, human beings learn—and develop—through a procedure of trial-and-error elimination: When we confront mistakes or errors in our knowledge or understandings (knowledge or understandings that we have constructed) we try again; we construct new understandings, better ones, that eliminate the recognized errors of the old.

In learning from our mistakes, the crucial step is the recognition or discovery of the mistake. How do we do this? Piaget helps us here, too.

DISCOVERING OUR MISTAKES: AGENCIES OF SELECTION

We have seen that the actions human beings can perform—sensory-motor acts, linguistic acts, and logical operations—create theories (what Piaget calls schemes and concepts). We use these theories to construct our understandings of the situations we encounter. This Piaget calls assimilation. But in addition to creating theories and constructing understandings, we also employ our actions and our theories to select or reject mistaken understandings. We use our actions and our theories to uncover contradictions in our knowledge, to discover our mistakes. Once we discover a mistake, we modify or reconstruct our theories. This Piaget calls accommodation.

Each theory a person creates provides expectations, or anticipations. Our sensory-motor theories (how-to theories, like grasping and pulling) provide perceptual expectations about what one will see if one looks, hear if one listens, feel if one touches, about what will happen if one pulls. Our language theories provide communication expectations about the response others will make when one says this, rather than that, about how people will respond to our signals, our expressions, and our descriptions. Our logical theories provide relational expectations: "if p is true, then q follows; since p is true, then q must be true, too." Or, "if q is not true, then p is false, too."

When the expectations provided by our theories do not hold up, when they are disappointed or contradicted, then we recognize that we have made an error. Our understanding is mistaken. This leads us to reconstruct our understanding, to try again.

Sensory-Motor Selection of Errors

When something does not look, feel, sound, taste, or smell as expected, we recognize that we have made a mistake in understanding that something. And when we discover we have made a mistake, we modify or change our sensory-motor behavior in an attempt to eliminate or overcome this contradiction between what was expected and what has happened: we spit out whatever has an unexpected taste, we cry out or start at unexpected sights or sounds, we clutch at or draw back from unexpected shapes, textures, temperatures.

During the initial (sensory-motor) period of cognitive development, children have a solely sensory understanding of the world they inhabit. In trying to make sense of the situations they encounter, infants use their sensory-motor skills both to reject false or inadequate perceptual theories and to create new ones. This is a procedure of trial-and-error elimination as they continually touch, taste, smell, listen to, and look at everything in their environment.

When something does not taste as expected, an infant (often after repeated trials) stops trying to suck or ingest it. In modifying its conduct, the infant is trying to overcome the contradiction between what was expected and how it tasted—trying, in other words, to overcome or eliminate his mistake or error. In this way, the infant modifies and so improves his understanding of the world he inhabits: the infant comes to understand that some things are not for sucking.

Here's Piaget's observation of the trial-and-error elimination of one of his children, Laurent, nine days after his birth;

Laurent at 0:0 (9) is lying in bed and seeks to suck, moving his head to the left and to the right. Several times he rubs his lips with his hand, which he immediately sucks. He knocks against a quilt and a wool coverlet; each time he sucks the object only to relinquish it after a moment and begins to cry again. When he sucks his hand, he does not turn away from it as he seems to do with the woolens, but the hand itself escapes him through lack of coordination; he then immediately begins to hunt again.[21]

Initially, the newborn baby's movements are random, but very quickly these become deliberate "trials" guided by the expectations inherent in the inchoate "theories" the infant has already created. Here is Piaget's observation of his son at the twenty-first day after his birth.

Laurent is already half asleep; his arms hang down and his hands are open (at
the beginning of the meal his arms are folded against his chest and his hands
are clasped). His mouth is placed against the skin of the breast about 5 cm.
from the nipple. He immediately sucks without reopening his eyes, but, after
a few moments, failure awakens him. His eyes are wide open, his arms flexed
again and he sucks with rapidity. Then he gives up, in order to search a little
further, on the left side, which happens, by chance, to be the correct side,
but the rotary movement which he thus gives his head results in making him
let go to the breast and go off on a tangent. In the course of this tangential
movement, he knocks against the nipple with the left commissure of his lips
and everything that happens would seem to indicate that he recognizes it at
once. Instead of groping at random, he only searches in the immediate neigh-
borhood of the nipple. But as the lateral movements of his head made him
describe a tangential curve opposite, and not parallel, to the curve of the breast,
he oscillates in space guided only by light, haphazard contacts with the breast.
It takes a short time for these increasingly localized attempts to be successful.
This last phase of groping has been followed by an attempt at insertion of the
nipple, while the lips open and close with maximum vigor; and noteworthy
also for the progressive adjusting of the tangential movements around the points
of contact.[22]

    As we have already seen, structural accommodation occurs only three
times in human cognitive development: first, at the beginning of what
Piaget calls the preoperational period during which children develop
linguistic structures by modifying or reconstructing the already existing sensory-motor structures; second, at the beginning of the concrete
operational period, during which children develop logical operations
(to perform on concrete objects) out of the already present linguistic
structures; and third, at the beginning of the formal operational period during which children develop logical operations (to perform on
propositions) out of the already present concrete logical operations.
    In the second kind of accommodation, which I call theory accom-
modation, the modification or construction of theories (concepts and
schemes) is endless. We can and do continually change and modify
the theories through which we construct our understandings of the situations we encounter. We can call theory accommodation learning,
thereby distinguishing it from structural accommodation, which usually is called cognitive development. Learning and development are
related insofar as the kind of learning one can have—that is, the kind
of theory accommodations one can make—depends upon the stage or
period of cognitive development one is in.

Language and the Selection of Errors

In the second period of cognitive development (the preoperational period), children begin to speak. Now they can engage in what Piaget calls representational thought. Through speech, children can construct symbolic representations of their understandings. So what we have, according to this interpretation, are (1) sensory-motor actions that create theories, which (2) we use to construct understandings, which (3) we now can make public through speech.

How does speech develop? According to Piaget, it is a matter of reconstructing or modifying the sensory-motor actions the child can already perform. What happens is that some of the sights, sounds, smells, and so forth that the infant makes or constructs cause problems. The infant sees food he cannot taste, hears sounds that frighten him, and so on. The agitation such understandings engender in the infant usually manifests itself in cries and noises of various kinds. These noises sometimes help the infant to solve his problem: adults fetch food for him or pick him up and console him, for example. Through trial-and-error elimination the infant, over time, modifies the sounds he makes in order to use these sounds to signal others and to express his understandings of the situations he encounters.

Here is Piaget's account of the trial-and-error elimination "gropings" of his own children in their initial linguistic acts:

At about 6, L. was becoming more and more skillful in using adults in order to obtain what she wanted, and always grizzled when they refused or pretended not to hear. One of her grandfathers was the person she found most accommodating, with the result that at I:6 (13) she began to use the term "panana" not only to call her grandfather, but also to indicate that she wanted something, even when he was not present. She would indicate what she wanted by saying its name, give a definite grizzle, and add "panana." At I:6 (9) she even said "panene" when she was finding it boring to be washed; "panene" was merely an indication that she wanted something to amuse her.

At I:3 (14) L. said "no" not only when she was refusing something, but when she failed to find something she was feeling for. The transition between the two senses was the "no" applied to a forbidden object. Similarly, the word "avoua," a corruption of au revoir, referred to people going away, herself going out of a room, touching a door, or merely getting up from her seat.[23]

The development of language initiates the child into a new world— the symbolic world, the world of culture, the world created by other human beings. Language exists apart from any human being, and it exists before human beings are born. Since this is a world of already established expressions and signals, a world of existing meanings, children must grasp that world: they must come to use language the way most people around them use language. This is, again, a matter of trial-and-error elimination. Here the child's language schemes or theories serve as the agency of selection. But because language is interactive, other people help him discover mistakes. More precisely, the responses that other people make to the sounds that young children make help the children learn from their mistakes.

A baby's first moves and sounds usually secure a response from others, especially from its parents: "listen to him," "he's happy," "he's hungry," "he's tired," "he wants his bottle," "he wants his Mama." This "feedback" helps children to discover and eliminate their mistakes. They learn how better to express themselves, how better to signal to others. And they learn this through trial-and-error elimination. If the parents respond incorrectly to a sound the child makes, or if they do not respond to it at all, the child tries again, modifying the earlier attempt in some way ("Wanna dinka wawa" becomes, after many trials, "I want a drink of water").

The earliest uses of language the infant develops are to signal and express. Human language, however, unlike animal language, is not used solely to signal or to express. Humans also use language to describe. The descriptive use of language develops as a modification of the earlier developed signal and expressive uses. That is, children now begin to make public their perceptual understandings of what things are— the sights, sounds, smells, and so forth that they construct of the situations they encounter. Descriptions are about objects outside of a child, whereas expressions and signals are about a child's needs, wants, desires, problems. Like all learning, learning what things are (descriptions) is a matter of trial and error, a matter of learning from mistakes. Here, too, the other people, usually adults, serve as feedback mechanisms. The responses of other people to the child's trial descriptions help the child to eliminate their errors. Note that with descriptive learning, adults provide feedback not only to the way the children formulate the sounds but to the content as well ("This is an apple, not a banana. *That* is a banana, not a 'bana.' Now say: 'apple' ").

Here is Piaget's observation of the early development of the descriptive use of language in his daughter Jacqueline:

At I:1 (0) J. used the conventional onomatopoeic sound "tch, tch" to indicate a train passing her window, and repeated it each time a train passed,
probably after the suggestion had been first made to her. But she afterwards
said "tch, tch" in two quite distinct types of situations. On the one hand, she
used it indiscriminately for any vehicles she saw out of another window—cars,
carriages, and even a man walking.

At about I:1 (6), and on the following days, any noise from the street, as well
as trains, produced "tch, tch." But on the other hand, when I played bo-
peep, appearing and disappearing without speaking, J. at I:1 (4) also said "tch,
tch" probably by analogy with the sudden appearance and disappearance of
the trains.

At about I:1 (20) she said "bow-wow" to indicate dogs. At I:1 (29) she pointed
from her balcony at the landlord's dog in the garden and said "bow-bow." The
same day, a few hours later, she made the same sound as she pointed to the
geometrical pattern on a rug (a horizontal line crossed by three vertical lines).

At I:2 (1) on seeing a horse from her balcony, she looked at it attentively
and finally said "bow-wow." Same reaction an hour later at the sight of two
horses. At I:2 (3) an open pram which a woman was pushing and in which
the baby was clearly visible produced "bow-wow." (This too was seen from
her balcony.)

At I:2 (4) she said "bow-wow" at the sight of hens, and at I:2 (8) at the sight
of dogs, horses, prams, and cyclists, "tch tch" being apparently reserved for
cars and trains. At I:2 (12) "bow-wow" referred to everything seen from her
balcony: animals, cars, the owner of the house (whose dog had first been called
"bow-wow") and people in general. At I:2 (15) the term was applied to the
trucks railroad porters were pulling, a long way from the house. At I:3 (7) it
again referred to the pattern on the rug. Finally, after I:4 "bow-wow" seemed
to be definitely reserved for dogs.[24]

In time, most children learn how to describe things correctly, which
is to say that they learn to use language to make the kinds of distinctions and the kinds of generalizations made by those people with whom
they have continual contact. It is true that children imitate the speech
of those about them. But imitation is a form of trial-and-error elimination, and the speech models children encounter serve both to elicit
and to regulate (identify errors in) the children's (trial) speech. Children do not *absorb* the language of those around them. Rather, those
around them supply feedback by responding (explicitly or implicitly)
to what children say, how they say it, and when they say it. They

help children to recognize their mistakes. And children modify their speech when others, by their responses, reveal its inadequacies.

After children learn *how* to speak, other people continue to provide feedback in regard to knowledge about the nature of things. Descriptive language reveals or makes public one's theories about the structures and organizations of things. When we use language descriptively, we classify, and we classify things according to our theories about what makes them what they are and what distinguishes one thing from another.

Here are some observations that Piaget made of his daughter, Jacqueline, during her preoperational period. We see how what she says reveals her theories about what things are, and at the same time we can see how adults provide feedback for her in the trial-and-error procedure she goes through in constructing and reconstructing her understandings of the nature of things.

> At 3:2 (20) we passed a man:
> "Is that man a Daddy?"
> "What is a Daddy?"
> "It's a man; he has lots of Luciennes and Jacquelines."
> "What are Luciennes?"
> "They are little girls and Jacquelines are big girls."
> J. at 2:6 (3): "That's not a bee; it's a bumble bee. Is it an animal?"
> At 3:3 (27): "Are little worms animals?"
> J. at 3:2 (23) could not understand that Lausanne was "all the houses together" because for her it was her grandmother's house, "Le Cret," that was "the Lausanne house." For instance, talking about a lizard climbing up the wall she said: "It's climbing up the Lausanne house." The next day, I wanted to see if my explanation had been understood.
> "What is Lausanne?" "It's all these houses" (pointing to all the houses around). "All these houses are Le Cret." "What's Le Cret?" "It's granny's house, it's Lausanne."[25]

In addition to using language to signal ("No!") and to express ("I want my bottle") and to describe ("This is a bumble bee"), there is a fourth use of human language: argumentation. The organum of argument is logic. This means that children cannot argue until they can perform logical operations, which, as we saw, usually begins about the age of seven. Before their concrete-logical period, children do attempt to argue, but their arguments have no logical cogency. Recall the example cited earlier when discussing causality when the child of 4:0 explained that the smoke in the funnel made the engine go. Or the child of 6:0 who said that the sun does not fall down because it is hot, or because it is yellow. Piaget calls the preoperational argumentative use of language transductive reasoning. The preoperational child juxtaposes or associates elements rather than connecting them logically ("I haven't had my nap, so it isn't afternoon").

Lacking the ability to perform logical operations, the preoperational child is incapable of recognizing contradictory propositions; hence cannot identify false claims or mistaken propositions on logical grounds. The only ways that preoperational children can uncover mistakes are through their sensory-motor actions ("I see it, it's a bumble bee") or through feedback from others ("Is a worm an animal?").

Logical Selection of Errors

Earlier we saw that once children develop the ability to perform logical operations they can create theories that logically cohere with one another, and they can use these theories to construct logically coherent understandings of the situations they encounter. In addition to creating better theories and constructing better understandings, the ability to perform logical operations enables them to identify and select out mistakes on "logical grounds."

You will recall that children develop these logical operations in two stages or periods. At about seven years of age, children begin to be able to perform logical operations on concrete objects. At about eleven years of age, they move beyond this concrete operational level and are able to perform logical operations on statements and propositions.

These logical operations are modifications or reconstructions of the linguistic acts children can already perform at the preoperational level. At the preoperational level, we saw that children can make distinctions and form generalizations about the nature of things ("All ducks are birds. Some birds are ducks"). But they make mistakes about the nature of things because they cannot perform logical operations and they cannot create relational theories. Piaget devised a brilliant experiment that reveals the kinds of mistakes preoperational children make when they encounter situations that can be understood only by performing logical operations on classes of objects.

A preoperational child (6:8) is given a set of wooden beads, eighteen of which are brown and two of which are white:

Adult: "Are there more wooden beads or more brown beads?"
Child: "More brown ones, because there are two white ones."
Adult: "Are the white ones made of wood?"
Child: "Yes."
Adult: "And the brown ones?"
Child: "Yes."
Adult: "Then are there more brown ones or more wooden ones?"
Child: "More brown ones."[26]

The preoperational child here depends solely on his sense perceptions and language acts to make sense of the situations he encounters. The child perceives and linguistically distinguishes wooden beads, brown beads, and white beads. But he cannot construe the logical relationships among these classes and subclasses of beads. An operational child, on the other hand, has no trouble with these logical relationships.

Adult: "Are there more brown beads or more wooden beads?"
Child (8:0): "More wooden ones."
Adult: "Why?"
Child: "Because the white ones are made of wood as well."[27]

Once they can perform logical operations, children possess a new and powerful agency of selection with which they can identify false or mistaken claims about the world. They can, for example, now reject as false the claim that the amount of water increases when it is poured from a fat, short glass into a tall, thin glass. They know that this claim is false because they now have a theory of identity that incorporates inverse relationships—a theory they created by the logical operations they can now perform.

Concrete operational children are less dependent upon adults as agencies of selection. They can figure things out for themselves. Or better, they use logic to identify contradictions. Not propositional logic, but concrete logic. As long as they can observe and manipulate concrete materials, they can test and refute most claims made about those objects ("This block of wood will float in water. That block of metal will not").

In addition to the logic of classes, concrete operational children can perform the logical operations of seriation. This involves correct use of terms like "smaller than," "larger than," "fatter than." To be able to seriate, one must be able to perform logical operations such that if A is larger than B (A > B), then one can reverse this to conclude that B is smaller than A (B < A); or, if in a series A > B > C > D, then, D < C < B < A. Piaget discovered that preoperational children cannot seriate. If they are given a collection of sticks graduated in length, they cannot arrange them in order according to length. They can pick out "big" sticks and "small" sticks but cannot employ the terms "bigger" or "smaller" with any consistency. Concrete operational children can seriate. They can perform this experiment with graduated sticks. But the concrete operational child makes mistakes, too. His ability to perform logical operations is limited and inadequate.

In a now classic experiment that reveals the limitations of the concrete operational stage, Piaget showed a child two sticks, one of which was a little longer than the other (A > B). Then, hiding the larger stick, A, he showed stick B and a still shorter stick, C (B > C). With A still hidden, the concrete operational child could not tell whether A was larger than C.

Concrete operational children make mistakes because they can only construct relationships among things that they perceive—concrete objects. As Piaget has noted, a concrete operational child "will agree that all ducks are birds and that all birds are not ducks. But then if he is asked whether out in the woods there are more birds or more ducks, he will say, 'I don't know; I've never counted them.' "[28]

Concrete operational children correctly understand that one can determine whether or not a given bird is a duck only by observing it. But then they mistakenly conclude that to ascertain if there are more ducks or more birds in the woods they will have to observe all of them. They cannot perform the logical operations on the propositions "all ducks are birds" and "some birds are ducks" that lead to the necessary conclusion that there are more birds than ducks.

In time, usually by eleven years of age, concrete operational children develop the ability to perform formal logical operations on propositions. This transition, like all cognitive development—from sensory-motor, to preoperational, to concrete operational—is a matter of learning from one's mistakes, a matter of trial-and-error elimination, a matter of groping. As we saw, the understandings that children construct in these earlier stages prove to be inadequate, false, mistaken; they lead to contradictions. To overcome the contradictions, eliminate the mistakes, restore cognitive equilibrium, establish cognitive order or coherence, children accommodate: they modify or reconstruct their actions or operations. These modified actions or operations then allow them to create new theories with which they can create new and better understandings of the situations they encounter.

This is not to say that once they reach the formal operation period children no longer make any mistakes. Far from it. However, operational children do now possess another powerful agency of selection with which to identify and weed out mistaken understandings that are presented in propositions. For any proposition formal operational children can construct its contradictions, and from any group of propositions they can draw implications. When they reach this stage of cognitive development, children are in a position to test each and every proposition presented to them or any propositions they themselves present to others. They test a proposition by looking for a true proposition that contradicts it. Thus, the proposition "all swans are white" is contradicted and refuted by the proposition "this is a black swan." Logic provides us with a powerful agency of selection, a tool for identifying false propositions—a means for learning from our mistakes, continually.

PIAGET AND EDUCATION

The interpretation I have presented of Piaget's work reveals that his principal contribution to the educational theory "we learn from our mistakes" consists of his conception of the learner as an active, fallible creator of knowledge who seeks order.

According to Piaget learners create knowledge, via actions and operations; they do not passively receive knowledge. The knowledge a person creates, however, is never perfect; it is always mistaken or inadequate in some way. We discover our mistakes through sense observation (sensory-motor actions), through oral and written feedback from others (language acts), or through logical deduction (logical operations.) These acts and operations serve as agencies of selection, by which

I mean that they reveal, or help us discover, contradictions to the knowledge or understandings we have created.

Because we seek order or coherence, we try to overcome or eliminate contradictions when we discover them. One way to do this is to construct new knowledge, new understandings, understandings better than the ones they are replacing because the new ones eliminate the contradictions discovered so far. Thus we improve our knowledge (learn or develop) through making mistakes.

A second related and equally important contribution of Piaget to the educational theory that we learn from our mistakes is his conception of cognitive development and learning: all cognitive development in human beings is a modification of actions or operations that a human being can already perform; all learning is a modification of existing learning, a modifiction of previously constructed understandings and/or created theories. These modifications take place in time, as the human being discovers the mistakes, inadequacies, and limitations of his existing performance and existing knowledge.

Thus the child is not a blank slate bereft of knowledge or understanding, as the transmission theorists would have him. Children—at the earliest age—have understandings; they are not empty vessels. As Piaget's work on causality shows (or as the work of Allan Funt with preoperational children on the old television show, "Candid Camera," also revealed), young children do have theories through which they make sense of the universe. Their theories are, of course, inadequate and erroneous. But this then sets the task of education. Education is a negative engagement; it consists of helping students to eliminate the mistakes inherent in their present knowledge. And the way to do this is to create learning environments, environments in which students can learn from their mistakes.

Piaget did no serious work in such educational planning. He did, of course, caution teachers about expecting children to learn things for which they are not ready or have not yet created adequate cognitive structures. And he made plain that the requisite learning environment will be one that allows and encourages activity.

I'm not an educator; I have no advice to give. Education is an area of its own and educators must find the appropriate methods, but what I've found in my research seems to me to speak in favor of an active methodology in teaching. Children should be able to do their own experimenting and their own re-

search. Teachers, of course, can guide them by providing appropriate materials, but the essential thing is that in order for a child to understand something, he must construct it himself; he must reinvent it. Every time we teach
a child something, we keep him from inventing it himself. On the other hand,
that which we allow him to discover by himself will remain with him visibly
. . . for the rest of his life.[29]

Other twentieth-century educational theorists have worked out the
role of the teacher in the formulation and development of learning
environments wherein children can learn from their mistakes, for example, Neill, Montessori, and Rogers, whose work I will analyze in
the second half of this book. In all cases, as we shall see, their conception of the role of the teacher presupposes Piaget's conception of
the learner as an active, fallible creator of knowledge who seeks order.

4

B. F. SKINNER

B. F. Skinner (1904–   ), a behaviorist, or, as he prefers to call himself, a radical behaviorist, is without a doubt the most influential American psychologist of the second half of the twentieth century. Behaviorism is usually defined as the science of human behavior. This science makes one assumption: that human conduct follows laws. Behaviorists say that they have discovered these laws by analyzing the systematic and functional relationships between the environment and the behavior of the organism.[1]

If we do understand the cause of human conduct, then we should be able to shape or change people to behave as we wish. And this, the behaviorists say, is just what education is all about: changing people—or, more precisely, changing behavior. To do this we must first of all know exactly how we want students to behave. We must have educational objectives—cast in the form of behavioral competencies. Once we have established the behavioral objectives, then we can employ the techniques of teaching based upon the science of behavior.

Behaviorists have taught pigeons to turn around, to pace the floor in the pattern of a figure eight, to stand still and stretch their necks, and to stamp their feet. They have also taught pigeons to bowl and to play a game of Ping Pong. Under the tutelage of behaviorist psychologists, pigeons have learned to peck at a red disk and to distinguish a red disk from a green one. And Skinner has boasted that behaviorists have "attained comparable results with rats, dogs, monkeys, human children, and psychotic subjects."[2] Human subjects have learned mathematics, spelling, logic, foreign languages, as well as social behavior—all by means of behaviorist teaching techniques.[3] Behavior modification does work.

THE CAUSE OF BEHAVIOR

What are the causes of behavior? In Skinner's view, there are no antecedent "inner causes"—no purposes, no needs, no drives, no motives, or anything else "inside the skin"—that explain human conduct. According to him, the causes of human behavior are the consequences of human behavior. Here we must be clear that Skinner accepts the fact that human beings are behaving organisms. So he is not out to explain human behavior itself but only to explain specific behaviors, behaviors that the person acquires, or learns; he is out to explain why someone does this rather than that. Most human actions, behaviorists insist, are learned behaviors.

But how can the consequences of behavior be the cause of behavior? All behavior has consequences, and some of these consequences, Skinner says, are reinforcing to the organism. Reinforcing consequences are consequences that increase the likelihood that the behavior those consequences are contingent upon will occur again in a similar situation. In a situation where we are thirsty, for example, taking a drink of cool water, beer, or soda will have reinforcing consequences. Those consequences will increase the likelihood that we will behave this way again in a similar situation. The consequences that are reinforcing—the contingencies of reinforcement—cause our behavior; that is, they cause learned behavior.

Again, take a student who receives a smile, a pat on the back, a kind word, or a high grade as a consequence of doing his homework. Such contingencies will reinforce this behavior, so he will be more likely to do his homework the next time the teacher assigns it.

A single reinforcement rarely suffices. Usually we need many reinforcements in order to learn a specific item of behavior. Reinforcement need not be continuous, however. It can occur intermittently in accordance with various timetables or schedules, based upon time intervals or upon response rates. It is the cumulation of reinforcement that conditions or causes behavior. Learning itself follows a "learning curve"; that is, all learning consists of an ever increasing rate of a response to a situation or a stimulus. The situation, or stimulation, that evokes a response Skinner calls a discriminative stimulus, and the behavior is said to come under its control. Reinforcers, therefore, cause behavior insofar as they increase the rate of response to the discriminative stimulus until finally the behavior is under the control of the discriminative stimulus. When this happens, the behavior is said to have been conditioned.

Human conduct, then, consists of behavior, and we acquire behavior as the result of reinforcement. A reinforcer is defined by its effect, not by any general characteristics. And effect refers to the increase in probability of the behavior upon which it is contingent. A piece of candy, say, is a reinforcer to a child not because it tastes good but only because it increases the probability of some behavior upon which it is contingent. (For some children, or for some children at some time, a piece of candy will not be reinforcing.)

Skinner distinguished positive reinforcement from negative reinforcement. Positive reinforcers are conditions that, when they follow behavior, increase the probability of that behavior being repeated. Food, praise, and so forth are usually positive reinforcers. Positive reinforcement works on pigeons, rats, dogs, and humans. Take a dog who is given food after a specific behavior. This food, when it follows or is contingent upon a specific behavior, increases the likelihood that the behavior will be repeated in a similar situation. And the more often this behavior is reinforced, the more likely it will become.

Negative reinforcers are conditions, the removal of which increase the probability of the behavior that removes them. Anything aversive to the organism is a negative reinforcer: pain, hunger, thirst, for example, are negative reinforcers. Behavior that removes or secures the escape from such conditions is likely to be repeated when the same conditions are present. A rat in a box, for example, standing on a metal grill through which an electric current is passing, will try to escape from the electric shock. If the rat presses the switch in the box that turns off the electric current, this negatively reinforced behavior (pressing the switch) is increasingly likely to occur again the next time the rat is in the same situation. And the more often the behavior is reinforced, the more likely it becomes.

Here we can note that Skinner regards punishment as the opposite of reinforcement. Reinforcement generates, or causes, behavior; punishment eliminates behavior. Punishment takes place when we remove positive reinforcers (taking candy from a baby because of [as a result of] his behavior) or when we impose negative reinforcers (slapping a child because of [as a result of] his behavior.) Skinner maintains that punishment is relatively ineffective in changing behavior. It is short lived and has undesirable effects, both in the punisher and the one being punished.

The reinforcement of behavior is a form of conditioning. Skinner calls it operant conditioning to distinguish it from traditional or respondent conditioning. Respondent conditioning begins with reflexive behavior, which is behavior like sneezing, yawning, blinking, and salivating. Everyone recognizes that certain stimuli elicit these reflexive behaviors: a tickle in the nostril makes us sneeze; a flash of light or an approaching object makes us blink; the sight or smell of certain foods makes us salivate. This is stimulus-response behavior: certain stimuli elicit certain responses. This reflexive behavior can become conditioned behavior. This happens when the response comes to be elicited by another different stimulus. Pavlov (1849–1936) conducted the most famous experiment in respondent conditioning when he conditioned a dog to salivate in response to a bell. He did this by ringing the bell just before giving the dog a chunk of meat. After many repetitions, the dog would salivate at the sound of the bell alone. As a result of the temporal association of the bell and the meat, Pavlov explained, the bell had become a conditioned stimulus: the bell elicited a behavioral response it did not naturally do before.

Respondent conditioning applies solely to reflexive behaviors and so cannot explain all of human behavior. For human beings do much more than sneeze, blink, and salivate. Indeed, most of human behavior is what Skinner calls operant behavior, the natural, ongoing behavior of the organism. It *operates* on the environment, hence the term, operant behavior. Operant behavior produces consequences. These consequences may be reinforcing or aversive, or they may be neutral.

Operant behavior always takes place in a context, in a situation. But situations do not *elicit* operant behavior as certain stimuli elicit reflexive behavior. (Reflexive behavior is part of our genetic endowment; we are born with this kind of behavior; hence, it can be elicited.) Operant behavior is an original response evoked by a situation to which a person has not previously been exposed. The situation does not elicit the behavior, the person *emits* the behavior in the context of a specific situation. When that behavior has reinforcing consequences, it is likely to be repeated in similar circumstances until, in time, conditioning takes place and that conditioned behavior thus becomes part of the person's repertoire.

SKINNER'S DARWINISM

Skinner's explanation of how human conduct develops is, he says, Darwinian. Darwin discovered the role of selection, which is a kind of causal explanation very different from the push-pull mechanism of science up to that time.[4] The principle of selection explained the origin of a fantastic variety of living things without recourse to purpose, or mind, or any antecedent cause. Just as Darwin used selection to explain the origin and development of the species, so Skinner says he has used selection to explain the origin and development of behavior.

Some behaviors were selected by the environment, Skinner says, because they were necessary for survival; or to put it another way, "Survival may be said to be contingent upon certain kinds of behavior."[5] If, for example, members of a certain species did not mate, care for their young, or defend themselves against predators, the species would not survive. These kinds of behaviors have become part of the genetic endowment of the species. They are what we call instinctive behavior. Instinctive behavior includes reflexive behavior, which as we saw above can become conditioned. Respondent conditioning is also necessary for survival, for this is how organisms adapt to their particular environment. As an example, Skinner points out that some organisms are born with certain cardiac reflexes. These reflexes support strong exertion, such as running away from or struggling with a predator. This reflex increases the organism's chances for survival. But predators vary in appearance, and it is only through respondent conditioning that a particular appearance can elicit appropriate cardiac behavior in advance of running or fighting.

Operant conditioning is also a matter of survival, a matter of the growth or development of behavior through selection by the environment. Many things in man's environment, such as food, water, sexual contact, and escape from harm, are crucial to survival, and any behavior that produces them will be selected. In the language of operant conditioning, these behaviors are strengthened by the consequences: "When a hungry organism exhibits behavior that produces food, the behavior is reinforced by that consequence, and is, therefore, more likely to recur. Behavior that reduces a potentially damaging condition, such as an extreme of temperature, is reinforced by that consequence, and therefore, tends to recur on similar occasions."[6]

The growth of behavior, then, like the growth of the species, is a matter of adaptation to the environment. But such adaptation involves no purpose, or intent, or aim on the part of the organism. It is solely a matter of selection by the environment.

THE TECHNOLOGY OF TEACHING

The scientific analysis of behavior provides principles that can be applied to education: to the design of schools, equipment, textbooks, and classroom practices. The principles of learning consist of three variables: a situation or occasion that educes behavior; the behavior itself; and the consequences of the behavior. The teacher must determine the behavior to be learned, must devise situations to evoke that behavior, and most importantly, must arrange contingencies of reinforcement.

Skinner has explained how a pigeon was taught to pace a figure eight.

A hungry pigeon is placed in an enclosed space. . . . A food dispenser can be operated with a hand switch held by the demonstrator. The pigeon has learned to eat from the food dispenser without being disturbed by its operation, but it has not been conditioned in any other way. The class is asked to specify a response that is not part of the repertoire of the pigeon. Suppose, for example, it is decided that the pigeon is to pace a figure eight. The demonstrator cannot simply wait for this response to occur and then reinforce it. Instead, he reinforces any current response which may contribute to the final pattern - possibly simply turning the head or taking a step in, say, a clockwise direction. The reinforced response will quickly be repeated (one can actually see learning take place under these circumstances), and reinforcement is then withheld until a more marked movement in the same direction is made. Eventually, only a complete turn is reinforced. Similar responses in a counterclockwise direction are then strengthened, the clockwise movement suffering partial extinction. When a complete counterclockwise movement has been shaped, the clockwise turn is reinstated and, eventually, the pigeon makes both turns in succession and is reinforced. The whole pattern is then quickly repeated, QED.[7]

The whole process should take no more than five or ten minutes, Skinner says. And during the whole of this time, the teacher's only contact with the pigeon is through the hand switch he uses to operate the food dispenser. By first identifying the behavioral objectives, he can then improvise a program of contingencies to reinforce that behavior, which gradually approaches the terminal behavior.

This method of teaching by shaping or modifying behavior is readily adapted to human beings, as Skinner reports:

A boy was born blind with cataracts. Before he was of an age at which an operation was feasible, he had begun to display severe temper tantrums, and after the operation he remained unmanageable. It was impossible to get him to wear the glasses, without which he would soon become permanently blind. His tantrums included serious self-destructive behavior and he was admitted to a hospital with a diagnosis of "child schizophrenia." Two principles of operant conditioning were applied. The temper tantrums were extinguished by making sure that they were never followed by reinforcing consequences. A program of contingencies of reinforcement was then designed to shape the desired behavior of wearing glasses. It was necessary to allow the child to go hungry so that food would be used as an effective reinforcer. Empty glass frames were placed about the room and any response which made contact with them was reinforced with food. Reinforcement was then made contingent on such activities as picking up the frames and carrying them about in a programmed sequence. Some difficulty was encountered in shaping the response of putting the frames on the face in the proper position. When this was eventually achieved, the prescription lenses were put in the frames.[8]

Skinner reports that after thirty days the child wore the glasses twelve hours a day—essentially all the child's waking hours.

In his book, *The Technology of Teaching*, Skinner suggests techniques for teaching writing, memorizing a poem, and teaching the meaning of words. All teaching is a matter of modifying or shaping behavior. In all cases, the teacher identifies the behavioral objectives, evokes the behavior, and arranges contingencies of reinforcement. A teacher can evoke behavior simply by giving the student verbal instructions or by presenting a model for the student to imitate or copy. Skinner calls this priming, as in priming a pump. Another form of priming is to prompt—to give the student a hint or a partial answer, just enough to evoke the correct answer. Reinforcers in the classroom can be candy, prizes, tokens, grades, honors, privileges, smiles, nods, pats on the back, and saying "right" or "correct." In addition, there are the automatic reinforcements of being right and moving forward.

Behavioral modification is difficult for the teacher to carry out, even if the teacher devotes all of his time to a single child. With a classroom full of students, the difficulty is multiplied many times. For this reason, Skinner suggests using mechanical devices, called teaching machines. Here material is "programmed" in the machines such that the student encounters one problem at a time and one problem depends upon the answer to the preceding ones. Progress through the program leads the student to acquire a complex repertoire. Reinforcement for the right answer is immediate, in the form of satisfaction with success and in the form of progression to the next more difficult or challenging step. Since the steps in the program are small, reinforcement is frequent.

In spite of what many people believe, programmed instruction can do more than teach facts and simple skills. It can also teach thinking. According to Skinner, thinking is behavior, whether in the form of paying attention, observing, making decisions, or solving problems. To teach thinking, the teacher must first specify the behaviors to be learned, evoke these behaviors, and arrange for contingencies of reinforcement. As to problem solving, for example, Skinner points out that "a person has a problem when some conditions will be reinforcing, but he lacks a response that will produce it. He will solve the problem when he emits such a response."[9] But solving a problem is more than *emitting* a response that is the solution. It is a matter of taking steps to make that response more probable. These steps are techniques, behaviors, which can be specified beforehand. Here are some of the problem-solving techniques we can specify:

If the problem is to say whether two things are the same or different, we may put them side by side to facilitate a comparison; if it is to make sure we shall treat them as different, we separate them. We group similar things in classes in order to treat them the same way. We put things in order if the solution requires a series of steps. We restate a verbal response by translating it from words into symbols. We represent the premises of a syllogism with overlapping circles. We clarify quantities by counting and measuring.[10]

As with teaching anything else, a teacher can specify these behaviors, then take steps to evoke them, and arrange for contingencies to reinforce them.

SKINNER'S LAMARCKISM

Although Skinner has claimed that behaviorism is Darwinian, he has constructed a transmission theory of education, probably the most comprehensive transmission theory in the history of education. When it comes to education, it is apparent that he abandons Darwin. He admits, "The parallel between biological and cultural evolution breaks down at the point of transmission. . . . Cultural evolution is Lamarckian in the sense that acquired characteristics are transmitted."[11]

Skinner is forced into Lamarckism at this point because of his "common sense" subjective conception of knowledge and culture. For Skinner, culture—and knowledge—is simply behavior. And behavior is something that people possess. Knowledge and culture do not exist apart from people. Knowledge and culture have no objective existence. A culture, Skinner says, is made up of how people live, how they raise their children, how they gather or cultivate food, what kinds of dwellings they live in, what they wear, what games they play, how they treat each other, how they govern themselves, and so on. These, he says, are "the customs, the customary behaviors of a people. . . . The practices of a culture, like the characteristics of a species, are carried by its members who transmit them to the other members."[12] As a transmission theorist, Skinner accepts the common sense view that knowledge is subjective, regarding knowledge as behavior and, therefore, as the personal possession of some subject.

Yet he does not view the learner as a receptor of knowledge, as do most other transmission theorists. As we saw, he claims that people create knowledge—at least, in a sense—insofar as they emit behavior. The organism is the source of knowledge. But this theory of the learner as an active creator of knowledge when it appears in the context of a transmission theory of education leads Skinner to construe education as an engagement of complete manipulation and total control. The teacher must determine what behaviors the student should learn, construct a situation that educes these behaviors from the student, and arrange an environment that reinforces the desired behaviors.

This emphasis on control has raised violent objections to the behaviorist position, as Skinner himself has noted. Yet he insists there can be no choice between control or no control. Human behavior is *always* controlled. If we teachers, parents, adults refuse to control the behavior of the young, refuse to see to it that they do develop proper behaviors, then we are abandoning them to adventitious control by contingencies of reinforcement—contingencies that may result in behaviors that endanger our very survival as a civilization. Although teachers do not like to admit that they are engaged in the control of behavior, they should, Skinner says, recognize that their role is just that.[13]

SKINNER'S DETERMINISM

At the root of Skinner's insistence on the inevitability of control in education lies the one assumption that behaviorists make about human conduct: that human conduct follows laws. For to view human conduct this way is to construe it as a process, something that goes on in accordance with causal laws. Behaviorists assume that human conduct—goings-on like taking a bath, tying a shoelace, reading a book—is in the same category as physical changes—goings-on like ice melting, balls rolling down inclined planes, planets orbiting. All physical changes are processes. They take place in accordance with causal laws. These changes are determined. So Skinner assumes that human conduct, like physical change, is determined. He recognizes, of course, that we cannot prove that human behavior "is fully determined" but adds that "the proposition becomes more plausible as facts accumulate."[14]

Yet Skinner's determinism raises a collection of contradictions that indicate that the behaviorist explanation of human conduct cannot be true. And this is precisely the first paradox. That is, if what Skinner says about human behavior is true, then what he says cannot be true. For Skinner says that all human conduct is the result of conditioning by the environment. But if this is true, then *what* Skinner said ("All human conduct is the result of conditioning by the environment") must also be the result of Skinner's own conditioning by the environment. And if all behavior is the result of conditioning by the environment, then we have no more reason to accept Skinner's verbal behavior as true than we have reason to accept someone else's verbal behavior as being true—someone who says that human conduct is *not* the result of conditioning by the environment. If behaviorism is true, we cannot take seriously as a reason or argument whatever is said in its support.[15]

A second contradiction comes from Skinner's attempt to explain exactly how behavior is determined by the environment. According to Skinner, "A response reinforced upon a given occasion is most likely to occur on a very similar occasion."[16] But "a very similar occasion" or "a similar condition" or "a similar situation" is, as we saw in chapter 2, only similar for *someone*. A repetition of a situation is *always* and *only* a repetition for a particular person or organism, simply because *all* repetition, *all* similarity, is a product of expectation in addition to the actual objective environmental conditions. (Remember the young puppies and the cigarette smoke?) This means that knowledge cannot be the result of conditioning since the very process of conditioning itself logically requires that the organism already possess that very knowledge supposed to result from conditioning. An example will make this clear. Suppose a child is confronted with an object, or a picture of an object, and behaves by saying "elephant." Suppose, too, that this behavior is followed by a smile from the parent, or a nod, or a "good boy!" or "wonderful!" According to behaviorist theory, on a similar occasion the child is likely to say this again. But to do this, to say "elephant" on a similar occasion, the child must recognize that it is a similar occasion. But if the child can *already* do this, then it already knows that this is an "elephant," which is what he is supposedly being conditioned to know.

A final contradiction emerges when Skinner attempts to interpret operant conditioning as an instance of Darwinian selection. To do this, he has to argue that there is a connection between reinforcement and survival. Skinner points out, for example, that sugar, salt, and sexual contact are necessary for survival. "As a result," he argues, "the human species, like other species, is powerfully reinforced by sugar, salt and sexual contact."[17] But such a contention leads to the conclusion that there is a preestablished harmony between organisms and the environment: we are reinforced by salt because it is necessary for survival. This not only flies in the face of all we know about the relation between organisms and the environment, it is also a conclusion that Skinner in another place explicitly rejects. "The notion of evolution is misleading," Skinner writes, "when it suggests that the good represented by survival will naturally work itself out." Things do go wrong, Skinner says, and "they may need to be put right by explicit design."[18] In advocating interference with the "natural working out" of selection, Skinner, of course, contradicts his claim that what reinforces organisms does so because it leads to survival. Skinner never solves this contradiction.

These contradictions reveal that determinism is false. Human conduct is not determined. Our behavior is not always and necessarily
controlled. But this is not to say that it cannot be controlled. In fact,
Skinner's work demonstrates that it is possible to create environments
where human conduct is controlled. Yet this does not mean that the
conduct is conditioned. But if controlled conduct is not conditioned
conduct, what is going on when conduct is controlled?

OPERANT CONDITIONING: A
REINTERPRETATION

In spite of the contradictions inherent in behaviorism, we must admit that operant conditioning does work—doesn't it? We can condition pigeons to peck at a red disk, to pace out a figure eight, and to
perform many other "behaviors"; and we can shape and modify human behavior, too. Can't we?

Yes, we can do what Skinner says can be done. But the theory that
purportedly explains why we can do these things is wrong. These
changes in conduct do take place, but they are not explained by
something called operant conditioning. We need an alternative theory to explain what is going on here. I want to argue the following:
conditioning does not exist. What looks like conditioning is actually
a matter of trial-and-error elimination. All learning is learning from
our mistakes. In short, I propose a Darwinian explanation for the growth
of behavior.

Yet you will recall that Skinner claimed that his behaviorist theory
was an instance of Darwinian selection. The trouble with Skinner's
claim, however, is that he equates selection with reinforcement; that
is, he says that the environment "selects" behavior by reinforcing it.
This converts Darwinian selection into a "common sense" process of
induction: repeated reinforcement is simply a repetition of the association of a specific behavior with specific consequences. These repeated associations, according to behaviorist theory, result in the acquisition of that behavior as a part of the organism's repertoire.

But Darwinian selection is not inductive. It is a matter of error
elimination: nature eliminates those organisms, or those behaviors, that
are unfit, inadequate, wrong. The growth of behavior or conduct follows the logic of error elimination. Growth always begins with an error, an inadequacy, a limitation—a problem. Problems arise from in-

adequate theories, or understandings—from ignorance. When we encounter a problem, we try to escape from it, eliminate it, or at least diminish it. Every problem is an instance of what Piaget called disequilibrium. Disequilibrium can be physiological, psychological, social, or cognitive. Pain, anxiety, disorder, and contradictions are all disequilibrating to human beings.

Disequilibration is aversive to us. This aversion is part of our genetic endowment. Those organisms that did not find pain—or hunger, or anxiety, or contradictions—aversive were not likely to survive. For such conditions as pain, hunger, anxiety, and contradictions are warning systems, signals telling us something is wrong, or inadequate, or missing. They tell us that we must change or modify our conduct or our understandings.

So when we are confronted with an aversive situation—which always arises out of our ignorance or our mistaken theories or understandings—we try to overcome that inadequacy by modifying our recognizably inadequate theories or understandings and, thus, our conduct. What we do is make a new trial. When that, too, proves to be inadequate, we eliminate that error and try again. In this way, our conduct improves—through a continual selection procedure of trial-and-error elimination.

Now trial-and-error elimination *looks like* reinforcement, especially what Skinner calls negative reinforcement. But there is no reinforcement going on. The environment does not reinforce behavior, it provides critical feedback to our conduct or our actions: it tells us when we have made a mistake, an error; it tells us when our conduct is inadequate. It is the organism that eliminates its errors, eliminates them in the new attempt, the new trial. When a hungry pigeon is put into a box, for example, it engages in exploratory trial behavior as it attempts to solve the problem of its hunger. As each trial peck the pigeon makes in search for food proves to be inadequate, the pigeon modifies its behavior on each successive trial peck. It eliminates each error by pecking someplace else. In the specially designed boxes Skinner uses for his experiments, only *one* (kind of) behavior will solve the problem: the pigeon must peck at the red disk, then it will receive food. According to my interpretation, the pigeon learns to peck at the red disk not because of so-called reinforcement but through a procedure of trial-and-error elimination as it attempts to solve the problem of hunger. This is a procedure of Darwinian selection.

In the same way, a child learns to read, write, spell, be courteous, tie his shoelaces, or whatever he learns: by trial-and-error elimination. The environment, or the teacher, or his parents do not *reinforce* his behavior; they provide critical feedback to his trials and efforts to solve his problems, his trial efforts to eliminate what is aversive to him. *

According to my interpretation, the organism modifies its own behavior through the selection procedure of trial-and-error elimination. No reinforcement occurs—ever. Operant conditioning is a myth. This is clearly the case in any instance of so-called negative reinforcement, where a hungry organism, say, goes through the procedure of trial-and-error elimination until it solves its problem, overcomes its pain. But so-called positive reinforcement is also a matter of trial-and-error elimination. In all cases of so-called positive reinforcement, organisms are trying to solve problems, overcome some perceived disequilibration. When someone tries to "condition" an organism by positive reinforcement, we have a very controlled environment where all conduct or behavior is erroneous, or mistaken, *except* that (kind of) behavior predetermined by the experimenter (controller) to be correct. In this controlled environment, the organism simply goes through a procedure of trial-and-error elimination until it hits upon the "correct" behavior.

But what about the programmed instruction materials that Skinner and other behaviorists have developed? Here it seems that the student does not go through any trial-and-error elimination because with these materials the student rarely makes an error. The programmed instruction material is so completely broken down into component bits and

---

*My use of the term "critical feedback" may convey the notion that human beings are actually transmitters and receptors after all. But this is because we usually construe critical feedback in the transmission mode of radio, television, and other media. In human transactions, however, critical feedback is presented, not transmitted, and constructed, not received. Thus, first the child *presents*, or displays, his present knowledge. The parent or teacher then *constructs* his own understanding of what the child has presented. Then, the teacher or parent *presents* his critical response. The child constructs his understanding of the critical feedback presented—and proceeds to modify his knowledge in light of this critical feedback.

Human beings are not radio or television transmitters and receivers, which never make mistakes. But we human beings do frequently misunderstand the knowledge that another displays or presents. We improve our understandings through continued interaction or dialogue.

so sequenced that most students can go through it without making any errors. And they learn the material.

What is going on here, I suggest, is that the student engages in the procedure of trial-and-error elimination "in his head." He makes no overt errors or mistakes because he has already "tried out" and "eliminated" tentative trial solutions before he commits anything to paper. It is like doing a crossword puzzle: we deliberately and consciously go through the procedure of trial-and-error elimination "in our heads" before putting a word down on the paper. With crossword puzzles, as with so-called programmed instruction materials, the context provides enough clues and feedback for us to ascertain whether or not a tentative trial answer is mistaken. This is manifestly clear in the following segment from a program in high school physics (see p. 88).[19]

The items, singly and cumulatively, provide a context that enables the student to go through fairly simple trial-and-error elimination in his head before writing down the answer. The first item sets the pattern. The student has to guess what word goes into the blank space. The context reveals that any word other than "bulb" would be wrong. In the second item, the context reveals that "battery" is the wrong word. By eliminating that, the student is left with the word "bulb." In the third item, the context reveals that he should eliminate all words not connected to "glow." The context also reveals that "heat" is the wrong answer. So he is left with the word "light." And so it goes. The student progresses through the "programmed material" by a procedure of trial-and-error elimination. The material is so easy—which means that it is so contextually rich in critical feedback—that he is able to conduct these trial-and-error elimination activities in his head.

This Darwinian explanation of operant conditioning helps to explain why it works and why it looks as though learning is a result of so-called reinforcement. This Darwinian explanation also helps to explain why behaviorism leads to the total control of students, to treating them like objects to be manipulated. Finally, this Darwinian explanation helps to explain why transmission is a myth, even though it seems to work. The learning of anything is always, in fact, a matter of trial-and-error elimination. Therefore, those who would try to "transmit" must control the environment of the learner in such a way that all trials except those predetermined as the "correct ones" must turn out wrong. In such a controlled environment, the organism is led inexorably to modify its own behavior through the procedure of trial-

Teaching Machines

Part of a program in high school physics. The machine presents one item at a time. The student completes the item and then uncovers the corresponding word or phrase shown at the right.

Sentence to Be Completed	Words to Be Supplied
1. The important parts of a flashlight are the battery and the bulb. When we "turn on" a flashlight, we close a switch which connects the battery with the ____.	bulb
2. When we turn on a flashlight, an electric current flows through the fine wire in the ____ and causes it to grow hot.	bulb
3. When the hot wire glows brightly, we say that it gives off or sends out heat and ____.	light
4. The fine wire in the bulb is called a filament. The bulb "lights up" when the filament is heated by the passage of a(n) ____ current.	electric
5. When a weak battery produces little current, the fine wire, or ____, does not get very hot.	filament
6. A filament which is less hot sends out or gives off ____ light.	less
7. "Emit" means "send out." The amount of light sent out, or "emitted," by a filament depends on how ____ the filament is.	hot
8. The higher the temperature of the filament the ____ the light emitted by it.	brighter stronger filament
9. If a flashlight battery is weak, the ____ in the bulb may still glow, but with only a dull red color.	
10. The light from a very hot filament is colored yellow or white. The light from a filament which is not very hot is colored ____.	red
11. A blacksmith or other metal worker sometimes makes sure that a bar of iron is heated to a "cherry red" before hammering it into shape. He uses the ____ of the light emitted by the bar to tell how hot it is.	color
12. Both the color and the amount of light depend on the ____ of the emitting filament or bar.	temperature
13. An object which emits light because it is hot is called incandescent. A flashlight bulb is an incandescent source of ____.	light

and-error elimination until it emits the "correct" response. Transmission does not exist, and anyone who attempts to transmit knowledge is doing nothing more than controlling the learner's procedure of making trials and eliminating errors.

By interpreting Skinner's behaviorism as a version of Darwinian selection, I have tried to show that Skinner, as interpreted here, provides a view of the learner similar to that of Piaget: the learner is an active creator of knowledge who seeks order (not reinforcement). Earlier we saw that the quest for order (what Piaget calls equilibration) takes place by means of eliminating contradictions. What Skinner has helped us to see is that we can use this notion of equilibration–disequilibration to explain all human conduct because equilibration occurs in other realms besides the cognitive: we can experience social disequilibration, physical disequilibration, and psychological disequilibration. What Skinner has also done is to point out that disequilibration is aversive to us, and this aversity to contradictions, pain, and anxiety is part of our genetic endowment; it is the result of natural selection.

If the learner is an active creator of knowledge who seeks order, then how is he to be taught? What is the role of the teacher?

PART III

How Teachers Can Help Students to Learn from Mistakes

5

MARIA MONTESSORI

Maria Montessori (1870–1952) was an intuitive pedagogical genius—a "natural." She constructed the most successful method of education in the twentieth century, perhaps the most successful in the history of education. In Montessori schools, children of three years of age learn to dust, to dry, to tidy, to set the table, to serve at table, to wash dishes. At the same time, they learn to take care of themselves: they wash, bathe, dress and undress themselves, they arrange their clothes in their locker or in a drawer, tie their shoes, comb their hair, and so on. By four and a half years of age, they learn how to write and how to read and can do basic arithmetic calculations.

The Montessori method works. Poor children and rich in all parts of the world have displayed this remarkable precocious intellectual development in the Montessori "Children's Houses" that have been established in most Western and a number of Eastern nations.

Montessori teachers all have special training. She herself designed a six-month international training course. Most courses are now a year long, some even three years. The training is both practical and inspirational. Prospective teachers learn that education is *not* a process of transmission, that their task is *not* to impart knowledge. Their role, they learn, is to release human potential: "To stimulate life—leaving it then free to develop, to unfold." Herein, Montessori wrote, "lies the first task of the educator." [1]

All prospective teachers spend a great deal of time in Montessori classrooms observing, practicing, and serving as interns. Among Montessori teachers, there is a rigid adherence to "the method" as laid down by Maria Montessori and made official (some say "sacrosanct") by the Association Montessori Internationale (AMI). The cultish atmosphere that surrounds her followers destroys the experimental approach that characterized Montessori's own work. [2] Yet this strict compliance with the exact methods as they were first set forth follows from the fact that Montessori herself had no theory of education. She was an intuitive genius who knew what the teacher must do to facilitate student growth, but she had no theory to explain why her method worked. Lacking such a theory, she could only tell teachers what to do, train them to follow punctiliously the method she herself used to facilitate growth. Without a theory that explains the method, teachers can do naught but follow the official method and teach according to the prescribed rules and directions. In this regard, it is noteworthy that there have been no significant changes or developments in the method for over seventy-five years, not since Montessori first formulated it. (When educators do attempt to modify and change the method, as happened in some American schools, the AMI declares them anathema and banishes them from the fold.) Noteworthy, too, is the failure to extend this method to upper elementary and high schools. When she did write about these upper levels of education, Montessori focused on the curriculum, claiming that the key to educational success lay with the correct "match" of materials, or subject matter content, to the interests of the students. Without a theory to guide her efforts, she could not adapt the pedagogical methods she had developed for younger children and so could say nothing about the role of teacher in educating older students. [3]

Yet there is a theory concerning the role of the teacher inherent in the Montessori approach to education, a theory that can enable us to expand the Montessori approach to all levels and all kinds of education. At bottom, the Montessori approach is Darwinian.

CREATING EDUCATIVE ENVIRONMENTS

The Popperian interpretation of twentieth-century educational growth I have presented so far has Piaget—and, to some extent, Skinner—

viewing the learner as an active creator who seeks order. According to this interpretation, we create knowledge by means of our theories, or cognitive structures, "making sense" out of the world as we encounter it. But because we are fallible creators, the knowledge we create is never perfect. This means that our knowledge can always be improved—it can grow.

Growth takes place via Darwinian selection. We uncover, or select, the mistakes in our knowledge, again, by means of our theories, or cognitive structures: we recognize or identify mistakes in our knowledge when they lead to contradictions. Contradictions are aversive to us, so after recognizing an error we seek to eliminate it by refining or reconstructing our knowledge.

The Montessori method presumes this conception of the learner. In *The Absorbent Mind*, she wrote:

Supposing we study the phenomenon of error in itself; it becomes apparent that everyone makes mistakes. This is one of life's realities, and to admit it is already to have taken a great step forward. If we are to tread the narrow path of truth and keep our hold upon reality, we have to agree that all of us can err; otherwise, we should all be perfect. So, it is well to cultivate a friendly feeling toward error, to treat it as a companion inseparable from our lives, as something having a purpose, which it truly has. . . . Whichever way we look, a certain "Mr. Error" is always to be seen! If we seek perfection, we must pay attention to our own defects, for it is only by correcting these that we can improve ourselves.[4]

The first step, Montessori goes on to say, is to recognize, or identify, our errors. Here we come to the key role of the teacher. Instead of "instructing" students, the teacher helps them to educate themselves: she creates an educative environment, an environment in which they can discover their errors and eliminate them—an environment in which they can learn from their mistakes.

An educative environment has three characteristics: it is free; it is responsive; and it is supportive.

A FREE ENVIRONMENT

By a free environment I mean an environment in which the learner is free—or feels free—to display, demonstrate, or make public his present knowledge. Most schools are not free in this sense. In most schools, students fear censure or correction because they are afraid of being judged, or graded, or compared with others. But in the Montessori Children's Houses the teacher does not punish, or correct, or evaluate. The teacher does not judge or evaluate the child's knowledge or compare one pupil's knowledge with another's. The Montessori classroom is a free environment, a place where the student is free from a "judgmental" teacher, a place where the student is free to disclose his present knowledge.

The teacher approaches the child in an invitational mode, encouraging him to talk, to act—to demonstrate his present knowledge, his present skills and understandings. Here is Montessori's method for teaching the young children the two colors, red and blue, by means of colored disks:

> She says, showing him the red, "This is red," raising her voice a little and pronouncing the word "red" slowly and clearly; then showing him the other color, "this is blue." In order to make sure that the child has understood, she says to him, "Give me the red," "Give me the blue." Let us suppose that the child in following the last direction makes a mistake. The teacher does not repeat and does not insist; she smiles, gives the child a friendly caress and takes away the colors.[5]

The lesson is brief, simple, and objective. By objective, Montessori means that the personality of the teacher does not enter the transaction between her and the pupil. The teacher does not cajole or coerce, does not display pleasure or displeasure with the child's present skills or understandings. The child is free from the domination of the teacher, free from the burden of trying to please her, free to display what he really knows, what he can actually do.

Because the teacher is neither fearsome nor threatening in any way to the students, she can evoke their present knowledge with facility. She can show and demonstrate skills and ask them to imitate her. They do so with alacrity—and impunity.

One of the gymnastic exercises the children perform, for example, is the "line." A line is described in chalk or paint upon a large space of floor. The teacher walks the line like a tightrope walker, placing her feet one in front of the other. she shows clearly how she sets her feet. The children imitate her without any necessity for her to speak. Montessori notes that "at first, it is only certain children who follow her, and when she has shown them how to do it, she withdraws, leaving the phenomenon to develop of itself."[6]

The children imitate one another, as well as the teacher. The absence of evaluation and comparison with one another creates a freedom for the children to try to do what others are doing. They are free to do things they want to do, free to try out their present abilities and skills. Take the case of the cylinders that the Montessori teacher uses for "sensory education." Here the teacher simply takes the cylinders out of the wooden blocks, mixes them on the table, and shows the two-and-a-half-year-old child how to put them back in the proper holes, but without performing the action herself. The child promptly begins to try to replace the cylinders, which are graduated in size, or in diameter, into their proper holes. Other children, seeing their companions at work, are encouraged to imitate them.[7]

The freedom in a Montessori classroom does not inhere solely in the demeanor of the teacher or in her manner of interaction with students. Indeed, the most striking characteristic of a Montessori classroom is that it is a children's house, a *casa dei bambini*. It contains furniture (tables, chairs, sinks, cabinets), it contains utensils (glasses, dishes, silverware), and it contains implements (mops, brooms, sweeps)—all of which are scaled down to the size of the little children. The small children can handle and use these implements and utensils; they can move the furniture about. Obviously, all this "invites" the children to imitate the activities performed by grownups. And this environment has none of the fears or constraints imposed by the normal "grownup" environment. In freeing them to perform these tasks, we can say that the environment evokes the children's present motor skills.

There are shoelace cards, button frames, and mounted zippers that the children use to try their hands at tying, buttoning, and zipping. There is also a wide variety of specially constructed "didactic materials" used to evoke the children's present abilities in sense discrimination: tubes, cylinders, and geometric solids of graduated sizes, shapes, colors, and weights, as well as various pieces of cloth and thread and paper of various textures, hues, and dimensions.

The children are free to do the exercises with these materials when they wish. There is no set order of lessons. The materials are like games to the students and thus provide a low-pressure environment in which they can demonstrate their present motor and sensory abilities and skills.

It is important to note that a Montessori classroom is highly structured. The didactic materials, the furniture and implements, all have specific functions and uses. They are not to be "played with" in any way the child may wish. Everything is specially designed to evoke the child's present knowledge, and each piece of apparatus usually evokes a specific skill. For example, there is a set of cubes for evoking the child's ability to discriminate size, a set of prisms to educe his ability to discriminate thickness, a set of rods to draw out his ability to discriminate length.

Although the teacher neither transmits knowledge to the pupils nor judges them, she nevertheless does *guide* them. Because the term "teacher" is so overloaded with the connotation of transmission, Montessori prefers to call the teacher a directress. The directress guides the child "without letting him feel her presence too much." The directress is always ready to supply *"desired* help" but never intervenes. The directress always respects the child and his present knowledge. She is calm. She waits—and observes. She allows the child freedom in his movements and his experiences.[8]

A RESPONSIVE ENVIRONMENT

The educative environment that exists in the Montessori classroom is not only free, it is also responsive. In this environment, when pupils freely display their present knowledge, they receive feedback to that knowledge, feedback that reveals the inadequacy of their knowledge, feedback that shows them that they have made a mistake.

As we saw earlier, there is a "natural" response to our knowledge in the form of natural consequences: if our motor skills are not coordinated, we bump into objects and knock things over; if our senses make inadequate discriminations, our projects go awry; if our language lacks precision, people fail to understand us.

The trouble with many "natural" responses to knowledge is that they can be harmful, especially to little children. Left to themselves to act freely in the world as it is, little children can suffer harm from the consequences of their actions: they can cut or burn themselves, fall, drink or eat something toxic. Because of their vulnerability to harm from the actions they might perform, we adults try to protect them by doing things for them, not allowing them to do it for themselves. We feed them, bathe them, dress them, undress them, carry them, hold them—all so that they will not "hurt themselves." In doing this, however, we prevent them from learning from their mistakes; indeed, we prevent them from learning how to learn from their mistakes.

The great significance of a Montessori classroom is that it is a specially created environment wherein little children can freely, and with security and safety, experience the consequences of their own actions. They receive critical feedback to their present knowledge.

Now every classroom does, of course, provide critical feedback to students. Usually this comes from the teacher: "That's wrong!" "You've made a mistake!" "This is incorrect!" But critical feedback from the teacher often frightens and inhibits pupils, especially if they are young children, which prevents them from freely demonstrating what they really know, what they actually can do.

In the Montessori classroom, the teacher is not the source of critical feedback (except for moral and social education, which I will discuss later). Instead, the critical feedback comes from the environment itself.

Motor Skills

In these classrooms, the chairs and furniture are light and easily moved. But this means that a child who is uncoordinated in his movements will tip a chair over or jar a table. This environment feeds back to him that his actions are inadequate. The child then has "evident proof of his own incapacity." Montessori notes that the same movement, had the child made it amid stationary benches or dishes "would have passed unnoticed by him."[9]

When he encounters such a consequence of his action (an overturned chair, furniture knocked aside), the child confronts a contradiction to what he had expected. This leads him to modify or change his actions in order to eliminate the inadequacies in his movements.

In this environment, where they can freely move about and directly experience the consequences of their actions, children of three and four years of age learn to walk and move about with care and grace. In this environment, they become accustomed to modifying their conduct in light of its unexpected consequences. They learn how to learn from their mistakes.

Montessori at one point recounts how in one of the children's houses in Milan the directress placed the little tables containing metal geometric forms on a low, narrow shelf. "The shelf was too narrow and it often happened that the children in selecting the pieces which they wished to use would allow one of the little tables to fall to the floor, thus upsetting with great noise all the metal pieces which it held." The directress asked the carpenter to change the shelf, but he was slow in getting around to it. Soon she discovered that "the children had learned to handle the materials so carefully that in spite of the narrow and sloping shelf, the little tables no longer fell to the floor."[10] Here was an unplanned instance of learning from mistakes. The environment was responsive: it "told" the pupils which of their actions were inadequate. And the pupils modified their own conduct in light of the errors the environment revealed to them.

Again, in the matter of tying shoelaces or buttoning and unbuttoning their coats and sweaters, we *could* allow young children to try do do this themselves. The trailing shoelace or the flapping coat would give them natural feedback, revealing to them the inadequacies of their skills. But dangling shoelaces could result in falls or spills, and unbuttoned coats lead to colds and sickness, so we perform these tasks for our small children. Moreover, it is *easier* for parents to tie the shoelaces and button the coats of young children rather than endure having them go through the process of learning from their mistakes. In the Montessori classroom, however, the shoelace cards and button frames provide the same kind of feedback to the children with no danger to them. And the directress is specially trained to tolerate patiently the children going through the procedure of learning from their mistakes. The child learns by trial-and-error elimination. "As he fastens and unfastens the same frame many times over with great interest," Montessori writes, "he acquires an unusual deftness of hand and becomes possessed with the desire to fasten real clothes whenever he has the opportunity." She reports that the smallest children learn—and want—to dress themselves.[11]

Sense Discrimination

Montessori was aware that critical feedback, as well as freedom, was an essential element in her method to facilitate growth. "The power to make progress comes in large measure from having freedom and an assumed path along which to go; but to this must be added some way of knowing if, and when, we have left the path."[12] What I have called

critical feedback she called "the control of error." Her didactic materials control the errors pupils make, making them manifest.

Each set of didactic materials is designed to select and reveal a specific kind of error. Take the cylinders, for example. There are three
sets of cylinders, each in its own block of wood. The first set has cylinders all of the same height, but the diameters diminish from thick
to thin. When the child removes them from the block of wood and
then does the exercise of trying to replace them in their proper holes,
they reveal the mistakes he makes in discriminating "thick" from "thin."
The second set has cylinders of the same diameter, but they vary in
height: this set discloses mistakes in discriminating "tall" from "short."
The third set of cylinders varies in both dimensions: they reveal mistakes in discriminating "large" from "small."

It is the responsiveness of these pieces of apparatus—the fact that
they have critical feedback built into them—that makes them didactic
materials. For this reason, Montessori insisted that the materials must
be used solely for the purpose designed. Children cannot use the blocks
of wood to build houses or make trains, for example, for then the materials would no longer be didactic: they would no longer reveal to the
student his errors and mistakes. Here is her description of how the
exercise used for the cylinders works:

He first makes trials; it often happens that he places a cylinder which is too
large for the empty hole over which he puts it. Then, changing his place, he
tries others until the cylinder goes in. Again, the contrary may happen; that
is to say, the cylinder may slip too easily into a hole too big for it. In that
case, it has taken a place which does not belong to it at all, but to a larger
cylinder. In this way, one cylinder at the end will be left out without a place,
and it will not be possible to find one that fits. Here the child cannot help
seeing his mistake in concrete form.[13]

The revelation of the mistakes provokes the child to eliminate his
error in another trial: "Before all the cylinders are fitted, now there is
one that will not fit. . . . He repeats the process again and again,
and finally he succeeds. Then it is that he breaks out with a smile of
triumph."[14]

Learning from Mistakes

With some of the materials, the control of error is within the child
himself. That is, the child must use his own sensory or motor struc-

tures to select and identify errors. The exercise in seriation, for example, has the child trying to order a set of rods that are graduated in length. Here the material does not control the error; the child must identify the error by sight.

In performing these exercises, many children make glaring mistakes, Montessori notes. In the light of Piaget's work on the stages of cognitive development, this is not surprising since seriation, as his experiments demonstrate, is an exercise that the child can peform only after reaching the concrete operational stage. In unwitting concord with Piaget's theory of cognitive development, Montessori says that the teacher must not intervene. The aim of the exercise, she explains, "is *not* that the work be arranged in the right order of graduation, but that the child should practice by himself." This brings out an important point about the Montessori method. When they do the exercise with the didactic materials, children are not solving *real* problems. Putting cylinders in their proper holes, or seriating rods are not problems anyone encounters very often in the real world outside school. Yet these exercises are meaningful and important to children. Through them they improve their abilities and skills.

Montessori recounts a scene she once observed in a public park in Rome, a commonplace scene familiar to many of us. A baby about a year-and-a-half old was shoveling gravel into a pail. His nurse called to him to leave. He continued shoveling. His nurse in exasperation filled the pail with gravel and set it and the baby into the carriage. The child loudly protested. The child, Montessori explained, did not wish to have a pail full of gravel. He merely wanted to go through the motions of filling it. (After filling their pails, most little children, as we know, dump out the gravel or sand and begin filling the pail again.) The child was trying out his skills, attempting to improve them. We also frequently see young children walking along the curb when the sidewalk is free and accessible to them. Here, too, they are trying out their skills, attempting to improve them.

The problems posed by the didactic materials used in the Montessori classrooms are important to children because they allow them to exercise and try out their skills and abilities: their intellectual abilities. Through them, they learn how better to distinguish this from that and how to perform logical operations like classification and relation.[15]

By developing his capacities and powers, his abilities to make distinctions, his powers to do things, the child "conquers independence." The essence of independence is to be able to do something for one's self. And in the Montessori classroom where the environment is both free and responsive, so that the child can display his present knowledge and receive critical feedback to that knowledge, the child becomes more and more independent. He is conscious that he is fallible but recognizes that he can improve. Here is how Montessori puts it: "The child might say, 'I am not perfect, I am not omnipotent, but this much I can do, and I know it. I also know that I can make mistakes and correct myself, thus finding my way.' "[16]

This independence, this heightened, conscious ability to learn from one's mistakes, is nothing less than adaptation to the world. We learn, or grow, through trial-and-error elimination. The Montessori classroom provides an environment that facilitates the development of this procedure. "The true function of infancy in the ontogenesis of man," Montessori wrote, "is an adaptive one; to construct a model of behavior which renders him free to act in the world about him and to influence it."[17]

Arts and Crafts

The free and responsive environment of the Montessori classroom facilitates other kinds of growth. In addition to improving their sensory and motor skills, children learn to write and to read, they learn basic arithmetic, as well as gardening and crafts, like drrawing and pottery making. In all cases, Montessori begins where the child is. The free environment invites the child to make public just where he is, what skills and abilities he presently has. Then, in various ways, the environment provides him with critical feedback so that he can modify, refine, improve his skills.

In teaching arts and crafts, Montessori teachers do nothing that is too different from the way many teachers teach their subjects. They use models and have children imitate them. As most teachers know, the presentation of models or prototypes for children to imitate is a way to evoke their present skills. Moreover, such models also serve as a check, as a source of critical feedback to the students. In drawing and painting, Montessori does use outlines of figures and pictures that the children fill in with colored pencils or paints (much like the present-day "coloring books"). This design exercise provides critical feedback in at least two ways: it discloses the child's muscular inadequacies in controlling a pencil or paintbrush; and it discloses his errors in observation. "One day," Montessori records, "a little boy, following one of our exercises in design, had chosen to fill in with colored pencils the outlines of a tree. To color the trunk, he laid hold upon a red crayon. The teacher wished to interfere, saying, "Do you think trees have red trunks?" I held her back and allowed the child to color the tree red. This design was precious to us; it showed that the child was not yet an observer of his surroundings."[18]

We cannot simply tell a child to observe, Montessori explains. As Popper would say, one must first have theories, or as Piaget would say, the child must first have a cognitive schema. To help the child create such theories, Montessori employs chromatic exercises. We already mentioned this exercise in the example of how the teacher helps the student to distinguish the colors red and blue:

"This is red." "This is blue."
"Hand me the red." "Hand me the blue."
(Later) "What is this?" "What is this?"

The set of chromatic materials consists of eight different hues of eight different colors. Each classroom contains two or more sets of these sixty-four cards so the children can do exercises in matching the colors from one set with those of another. After they have mastered the colors (developed their schemas, or theories), the children spontaneously apply these schemata or theories to the world about them. In the case of the child who continually colored the tree trunks red, the chromatic exercises worked: "He one day chose a brown pencil with which to color the trunk, and made the branches and leaves green. Later, he made the branches brown also, using green only for the leaves."[19]

Montessori schools usually have a garden attached. Here the young pupils learn to take care of and tend to plants. In the matter of learning how to garden, we find that nature provides critical feedback. That is, plants will not grow if they are not watered, or if they receive insufficient cultivation, or if they have not enough nutrients from the soil. The plants themselves, then, respond to the actions of the young gardener: they tell him what mistakes he has made. Learning how to garden, like all learning, is a procedure of trial-and-error elimination.

Language: Writing

Like gardening, the activity of using language (or "languaging," as Neil Postman calls it[20]) has critical feedback built into it. Human beings interact by means of language, which means that another's responses or reactions to what we say constitutes a form of critical feedback to what we have said or how we have said it. It is through critical feedback to his own trials in using language that the child has learned to talk. By the time he arrives at the Montessori school, the child has already learned the first of two functions of language: to signal and to express.[21] What the teacher concentrates on is having the child learn the descriptive function of language. Montessori calls this nomenclature. The exercises employed in teaching nomenclature all have a common pattern. Through questions and requests, the teacher evokes responses and reactions from the student. Once again, the exercise used in teaching color discrimination serves as the paradigm:

Demonstration:	This is red. This is blue (thick-thin; smooth-rough).
Request:	Hand me the red. Hand me the blue (thick-thin; smooth-rough).
Question:	What is this? What is this?

Because language, or "languaging," is interactive, both the student and the teacher get critical feedback through these exercises. The student's responses and reactions serve as critical feedback to the teacher's trial effort to facilitate the child's ability to understand and use descriptive language. But at the same time, the *teacher's* reaction and response to what the student says or does provides the student with critical feedback to his own actions. Recall that Montessori said that if the child makes a mistake then "the teacher does not repeat and does not insist; she smiles, gives the child a friendly caress and takes away the colors.[22] Now, this conduct of the teacher does, of course, provide the child with critical feedback. He does usually recognize that he has made a mistake. Yet, *at the same time*, the absence of prodding, coaxing, or correcting, the absence of any adverse comment or sign from the teacher, also reveals to the student that it is all right to make mistakes. (More on this later.)

We use descriptive language to select aspects of our environment—

to observe. First, we create the term or label (which is a kind of theory), and then we *match* the label to phenomena in our environment. This takes place spontaneously. Montessori reports how one day a four-year-old running about in the court suddenly stood still and cried out, "Oh, the sky is blue!" and stood for some time looking up into the blue expanse of the sky. Again, she tells how the children would sometimes gather about her and begin lightly caressing her hands and clothing saying: "It is smooth." "It is velvet." "This is rough."

The most remarkable part of language learning in a Montessori classroom is how children learn to read and write. Here, as always, it is a matter of creating a free, responsive environment wherein the child can learn from his mistakes, via trial-and-error elimination.

In teaching writing, there are three stages or exercises: first, the child improves his muscular control and motor movements used in writing. Here the exercise consists of stencils of geometric figures which the child first traces and then fills in with a colored pencil or a crayon. The outline helps the child to recognize how well or how inadequately he can handle the crayon, how well he stays within the outline. Then, he modifies his actions in light of its revealed inadequacies—and thereby improves.

The second stage of learning how to write has the child learning the letters, the *sounds* of the letters. Here the material consists of cardboard letters covered with sandpaper. The child traces the letters with his fingers, pronouncing each one as he traces it. The rough surface of the letters provides critical feedback to the child, telling him if and when he has made a mistake in forming the letter.

The final exercise is the composition of words. Once again, the material consists of cut-out cardboard letters, which the child uses to compose words that the teacher dictates: mama, papa, and so forth. The critical feedback in this dictation exercise is the completed word itself: the child knows the sound of each letter, so when he "sounds out" the word he has composed and it does not match the sound dictated by the teacher, he knows he has made a mistake. Montessori recounts how a Professor DiDonato, while on a visit to the Children's House, pronounced his own name for a four-year-old child. "The child was composing the name, using small letters and making it all one word, and had begun thus—*diton*. The professor at once pronounced the word more distinctly: di *do* nato, whereupon the child, without scattering the letters, picked up the syllable *to* and placed it to the side, putting *do* in the empty space. He then placed an *a* after the *n* and taking up the *to* which he had put aside, completed the word with it.[23] This four-year-old child, when the word was pronounced more clearly, understood that what he had composed did not match. He revised his first trial.

In none of these three exercises does the child actually write. Writing comes, in Montessori's words, as a "spontaneous explosion." Here is her description of this dramatic event in the first of the Children's Houses.

One beautiful December day when the sun shone and the air was like Spring, I went up on the roof with the children. They were playing freely about, and a number of them were gathered about me. I was sitting near a chimney and said to a little five year old boy who sat beside me, "Draw me a picture of this chimney," giving him, as I spoke, a piece of chalk. He got down obediently and made a rough sketch of the chimney on the tiles which formed the floor of the roof terrace. As is my custom with little children, I encouraged him, praising his work. The child looked at me, smiled, remained for a moment as if on the point of bursting into some joyous act, and then cried out, "I can write! I can write!" and, kneeling down again, he wrote on the pavement the word "hand." Then, full of enthusiasm, he wrote also "chimney," "roof." As he wrote, he continued to cry out, "I can write! I know how to write!" His cries of joy brought the other children, who formed a circle about him, looking down at his work in stupified amazement. Two others of them said to me with excitement, "Give me the chalk. I can write, too." And, indeed, they began to write the various words: mama, hand, John, chimney, Ada.[24]

Language: Reading

Reading, in the Montessori approach, comes after writing. Whereas writing is the transcription of sounds, reading is the interpretation of the meaning of phrases. Before he can interpret the meaning of phrases, the child must first learn to "read" words. He does this by pronouncing ever more rapidly written descriptive words for objects he is already familiar with. Say the written word is "hand." The child translates the written word slowly into sounds: h-a-n-d. He does this over and over, faster each time, until finally "the word bursts upon his consciousness." Then, Montessori says, "he looks upon it as if he recognized a friend."[25] This, too, is a matter of critical feedback, trial-and-error elimination. For the child already knows the word for hand as well as the descriptive terms for many other objects. When he makes trial "soundings out" of a written word, he matches or checks these trials against the words he knows how to speak. As long as the word sounded out does not match any word he knows, the child recognizes he is making a mistake in "reading" the word—it makes no sense, it has no meaning for him.

The passage from reading words to reading phrases is a long one. Children who can read words so that they are able to read shopping lists and read the names of objects from cards used in the classroom do not know how to read. They cannot read a book. They have only a mechanical ability to translate graphic signs into the sounds of a word they recognize. They do not construe written language as a means of communication.

To facilitate the passage from reading words to reading phrases, writing must, once again, precede reading. That is, before the child can read written phrases, he must first compose written phrases. Montessori reports that in the first Children's House, one day during a free conversation period, *four* children arose at the same time and with expressions of joy on their faces ran to the blackboard and wrote phrases on the order of the following: "Oh, how glad we are that our garden has begun to bloom."[26]

These children had arrived spontaneously at the art of composition, just as they had spontaneously written their first word. Following this, Montessori could communicate to the children by means of writing. She wrote questions on the board. The children read them and responded. She wrote requests. Again the children read them and reacted. The children had learned that written language can be used to transmit thought.

Reading and writing are mechanisms for improving our knowledge and our understandings. They are means for securing critical feedback to our present knowledge. They greatly facilitate the procedures of trial-and-error elimination by which our knowledge grows. At the same time, as we have seen, reading and writing are themselves the result of trial-and-error elimination. We learn to write and we learn to read by making mistakes.

Arithmetic

In teaching arithmetic, the Montessori teacher creates a free, responsive environment. As they learn everything else, children learn arithmetic through a procedure of trial-and-error elimination. Because it is a closed system, arithmetic can readily be incorporated into didactic materials, materials that provide critical feedback, revealing errors.

The best example of didactic materials for teaching arithmetic are the cuisinaire rods. These consist of ten rods of graduated length from a decimeter to a meter, with each rod divided into painted sections a decimeter in length. Each rod is called by the number it represents. Thus, the one-decimeter rod is called one, the two-decimeter rod two, the three-decimeter rod three, and so on up to ten. Using these rods, children can learn how to add, subtract, divide, and multiply.

Here's how it works. The students are asked to conjecture how to make a "ten" by using the other rods. Then they take up the rods to check their conjectures. To make ten, they put together (add) the one rod and the nine rod, or the two rod and the eight, or the three and the seven, and so on. They they are asked to conjecture what will remain if they take away a rod. Once again, they use the rods to check their conjectures. They see that if they take away (subtract) the one from the composed ten, a nine remains, take away two and eight remains, and so on. The rods provide critical feedback to their conjectures.

They learn multiplication by conjecturing how many twos make ten, how many fours make eight, and so on. Then they check their conjectures by rotating the two rod alongside the ten rod. As to division, the teacher asks how many twos are in ten. The children once again check their conjectures by manipulating the rods.

There is not too much arithmetical learning in a Montessori school primarily because the children there are so young—most are still in the preoperational and concrete operational stages. Yet the Montessori method could be readily employed with teaching older children arithmetic, children who have reached the formal operational stage.

The system of arithmetic, because it is a closed system, has critical feedback built into it. This means that arithmetical calculations are, or can be, didactic exercises. Thus, as they move beyond the concrete operational stage into the formal operational stage, children can perform these exercises with numbers themselves, without the rods or any kind of concrete apparatus. Given a problem of calculation, formal operational children can make a conjecture and also make a trial-and-error calculation. Then they can use the converse process to check their results, getting critical feedback to uncover their mistakes. Thus, if they add two numbers, they can check their result by subtracting one of the numbers from the total. After multiplying two numbers, they can check their result by dividing the product by one of the numbers multiplied.

EXTENDING THE MONTESSORI APPROACH

Teachers can extend the Montessori approach to older students and to all subjects. In all cases, the teacher can create a free, responsive environment wherein students can engage in trial-and-error elimination, learning from their mistakes. Many who teach skills or skill subjects—especially artistic skills and athletic skills—already do this. In some cases, specially constructed didactic materials may help, although in most cases the student can experience the "natural" consequences of trial performance and observe therein his mistakes and errors. (Photographs, films, and tape recordings of the student's performance can help facilitate the discovery of errors.)

In advanced subjects like science, history, and literature, which consist of knowing "that" rather than knowing "how," teachers can also employ the Montessori approach of constructing free, responsive environments. Learning these subjects consists of learning propositions: about the universe, about human beings, about the past. There is a logic to each of these subjects such that the propositions that make it up cannot be contradictory. It is this "logic" of a subject matter that allows the teacher to construct it into didactic material.

For purposes of teaching history, say, or physics, the teacher constructs an agenda. The agenda consists of problems or situations drawn from the discipline. The teacher presents this agenda to the students. They are not expected to receive it or master it but to encounter it, to respond to it, to criticize it. In responding, they disclose their own understandings, their own theories. Thus, the presented subject matter evokes or educes the student's own knowledge. A history lesson evokes the student's present understanding of the past; a physics lesson evokes his present understanding of the physical universe.

Teachers of these kinds of subjects can adopt a "Socratic approach" to teaching. After evoking the students' present understandings and theories, the teacher gives them critical feedback so that the students can uncover the errors or inadequacies in their present knowledge. The critical feedback can take the form of having students perform experiments to test their scientific theories, or it can take the form of having them do library research to check their theories about the past. More often than not, critical feedback can come in the form of an argument from the teacher: "You say that A is the case. And if so, then B follows. But B is false. Therefore, A cannot be true."

This critical feedback, however, should merely be the opening move in a critical dialogue, a dialogue between competing theories. For experiments can never be final, research never exhaustive, and arguments never conclusive, in any of these disciplines. So the critical feedback the student receives to his theories should lead him to construct counter-criticisms. The "critical dialogue" goes on until a criticism holds up to counter-criticism. This leads to a refinement or change or modification in light of the unrefuted criticism.

The critical dialogue that takes place in school usually reveals that the propositions or theories put forth by students are the ones most in need of modification or refinement. (Sometimes, however, the students' criticisms do reveal inadequacies in the theories accepted by experts in the field.) At any rate, students learn (or knowledge advances) through trial-and-error elimination.

In these critical dialogues, it may appear that the teacher is telling the student that he has made a mistake, thus contradicting the Montessori dictum that the teacher should not do this. But in a critical dialogue it is the subject matter—the logic of the subject matter—that reveals the errors in the student's knowledge. Just as the cylinders and the block of wood provide critical feedback to the young pupil's trial efforts in making sense discriminations, so it is the logic of the subject matter of physics, say, that provides critical feedback to the older student's theories about the physical universe. The teacher merely helps to make the contradictions manifest, or helps the student to discover the logical implications of his theories.

Yet critical feedback—in any form—can scare students of any age. It can intimidate them; it can turn them off. This brings us to the third aspect of an educative environment.

A SUPPORTIVE ENVIRONMENT

In addition to being free and responsive, an educational environment is supportive. When students confront mistakes in their present knowledge, they often get upset, dismayed, frightened, anxious. And then, instead of trying to modify or change their knowledge, they can become dogmatic—or they can even regress. A supportive environment can prevent this. It helps students to try again, to continually modify their knowledge in light of its discovered errors.

The Montessori classroom is a supportive environment. It provides support for the child in at least three ways: through the physical environment, itself, through the role of the teacher, and through the conception of education as Darwinian growth that underlies the operation of the classroom.

Physical Support

The Montessori classroom is a "Children's House," a place where the furniture, the utensils, and the implements of daily life are all scaled down to the size of the small children. Earlier we saw that in such an environment the children can move about freely. The environment frees the children, evoking their present motor and sensory abilities as they sweep and dust, wash and dry, clean and polish. The child-sized environment is also more responsive than the normal adult environment: it provides children with critical feedback, which leads them to modify and improve their skills and abilities.

But in addition to being more free and responsive, this special physical environment gives the children more assurance, more confidence—they find it supportive. Montessori reports that she had expected children to find joy and delight in this specially constructed environment, but she discovered that even beyond this "the child's whole personality changed. When the child was placed in this world of his own size, he took possession of it. He asserted his independence—as if he were saying, 'I want to do everything myself. Now, please don't help me.' "[27]

If the child becomes independent, then necessarily the role of the teacher must change.

The Supportive Teacher

Earlier we saw that in the Montessori classroom the teacher becomes a "directress," someone who guides the child's autonomous learning.

I explained that the role of the Montessori directress was twofold:

first, to evoke the student's present knowledge; and second, to help the student discover the errors or inadequacies in his knowledge. To do this, she focuses on the classroom environment, trying to make it educative: free, so that the child will make public his present knowledge; and responsive, so that the child will obtain critical feedback to his present knowledge.

In creating a free environment, the teacher eschews many of the traditional didactic moves that most teachers make. She does not compel, coerce, or cajole. Nor does she push, pull, or prod. Nor does she compare, condemn, or judge. The child is free from an adult who wants to "instruct" him.

In creating a responsive environment, the teacher avoids intervention. She does not correct the child, does not tell him he has made a mistake. It is not she who gives the child critical feedback, it is the environment and the specially constructed apparatus and materials. When the child is doing the exercise with the cylinders, for example, and ends up with one cylinder that will not fit into the single remaining hole, he needs no teacher to tell him he has made a mistake; the material "tells" him this.

Making a mistake does not worry or frighten the child. He recognizes that the teacher's care for him, her affection, her love, is *not* contingent upon his doing the exercise correctly or upon his giving correct answers. Recall, once again, the lesson with the red and blue disks: if the child makes a mistake, "the teacher does not insist; she smiles, gives the child a friendly caress and takes away the colors." I noted earlier that the teacher's reaction here does usually reveal to the child that he has made a mistake, but this very reaction—at the same time—makes clear to him that the mistake does not cause the teacher to withdraw support. So we see that in addition to the two roles of educing the child's present knowledge and helping him discover his mistakes, the third role of the Montessori teacher is to be continually supportive. (I should add that if the Montessori approach is used in teaching older students—high school, college, and graduate students—as I think it can and should be, the teacher will be less concerned with the role of providing support and more concerned to function as a critic, providing students with critical feedback.)

The model for the supportive teacher is the valet. "The valet keeps his master's dressing table tidy, puts the brushes in place, but he does not tell his master when to use the brushes; he serves the meals but does not oblige his master to eat; having served everything nicely, without a word, he disappears."[28] Likewise the teacher: the teacher must serve the child, but the teacher does not serve the child's body—washing him or dressing him, for example. The child must do these things for himself. The child acquires independence by becoming self-sufficient in these matters. The teacher serves the child's spirit, helping him to act, to will, to think for himself. By being supportive, the teacher does not make the child dependent on her. Instead, her support helps to launch him into self-sufficiency.

Conceptual Support

To be a supportive teacher, one must understand the educational engagement as a procedure of Darwinian growth. And this conception must be shared with the student. Here I am going beyond Montessori, for Montessori herself was not conscious that her approach embodied a Darwinian theory of education. So she never made these conceptual foundations of her approach a part of the explicit supportive framework of the classroom. (Montessori does talk about the "spirit of man" unfolding in some mystical fashion. She even talks about this in the language of the now discredited "vitalistic" theory of evolution.[29] But she never makes this an explicit part of the educational environment of the classroom.)

According to my interpretation of Montessori, there is a Darwinian theory of education inherent in her approach. This notion of Darwinian educational growth includes a conception of the role of the teacher, a conception of the nature of the pupil, and a conception of the content of education. Students are reassured by these conceptions. Sharing them with them makes the environment more supportive. In the Montessori classroom, the teacher does not transmit knowledge to pupils—she does not "teach." Nor does she evaluate, judge, or grade pupils. The role of the teacher is to create an educative environment: an environment that is free, responsive, and supportive. In this environment, pupils learn from their mistakes. And that's what schools are: places for making mistakes.

In the Montessori classroom, pupils are treated as active creators of knowledge rather than as passive receptors. They are not expected to "learn," "absorb," "cover," or "master" a predetermined body of knowledge but simply to improve their present knowledge: to get better. To "get better" means to make fewer mistakes. And getting better—improvement—is endless.

Growth is measured historically, not teleologically. By this I mean that growth is measured not by comparison with some end (or *telos*) but by comparison with what was present at an earlier point in time. In learning to write, for example, there is no predetermined standard of "knowledge of writing" by which we measure the growth of a student's knowledge of writing. Instead, we measure his growth by measuring how much he knows *now* in comparison with how much he knew *before*. (We measure how many fewer mistakes he makes now than he made before.)

Although Montessori herself never mentions it, the historical conception of growth permeates the Montessori classroom. Montessori students have no educational goals or aims. They are simply trying to improve their performance in successive trials, whether this is in the area of sense discrimination, in gardening, in drawing, in writing, or whatever. In this historically rooted educative environment of the Montessori classroom where the teacher never burdens students with telling them what they are going to learn, students come to believe that they are learning by themselves, as, in truth, they are: the teacher is merely the facilitator. When asked, "Who taught you that?" the student in the Montessori classroom usually replies, "I learned it by myself."[30]

MONTESSORI'S AUTHORITARIANISM

My Darwinian interpretation of the Montessori method as the creation of an educative environment—free, responsive, and supportive—wherein children can learn from their mistakes through the procedure of trial-and-error elimination is contravened by her approach to moral and social education. For in these realms, the role of the Montessori teacher is to impose predetermined modes of conduct on children. At this point, the Montessori approach becomes authoritarian.

This authoritarianism appears as paternalism in the earliest reports of her work with children of the poor in Rome. In an "inaugural address" she delivered at the opening of one of the first Children's Houses in a tenement building, she spoke of the directress as a "true missionary, a moral queen among the people." In this address, she insisted that the parents "must learn to *deserve* the benefit of having within the house the great advantages of a school for their little ones."[31]

Among the rules and regulations she established for the Children's House was the obligation upon the parents "to show the greatest respect and deference toward the Directress and toward all persons connected with the Children's Home." If parents failed to do this, their children were expelled.[32]

In her approach to teaching "discipline," Montessori starts off in a Darwinian way by pointing out that the young child's disorderly acts are actually his groping quest for order. The young child's natural quest for order—via crawling, creeping, squirming, touching, feeling, grasping—when prevented or interfered with, makes the child rebel. And the rebellion, Montessori says, "forms almost the whole of his naughtiness."[33] Instead of useless attempts to reduce the child to immobility ("Keep still!" "Be quiet!" "Don't touch!"), the Montessori classroom frees the child to encounter a responsive environment that helps him to improve his actions, helping him to move toward the order "toward which his efforts are actually tending."[34]

Once these little children can order their own actions, there emerges a "spontaneous discipline," a calm and an orderliness that make their movements not only effective but actually graceful. At this point, they disclose a love of work, something no one expected of them. They take up tasks and engage in constructive activities. Once their movements become ordered, they dust and sweep the classroom, they wash and dry dishes, they set and wait on tables at mealtime. Four-year-old "waiters" and "waitresses" take the knives and forks and spoons and distribute them to the different places; they carry trays holding as many as five water glasses; and finally, they go from table to table carrying big tureens full of hot soup. "Not a mistake is made, not a glass is broken, not a drop of soup is spilled."[35]

The structured environment of the Montessori classroom provokes the development of this remarkable self-control. But Montessori wants more than this. She insists upon the development of a collective discipline, a cohesion of the entire class of children in a group morality. In explaining this, she refers to the "collective interest," which for her takes the form of "good breeding." To instill "good breeding" the teacher must, she insists, "check in the child whatever offends or annoys others, or whatever tends toward rough or ill-bred acts."[36]

At this juncture Montessori is in a quandary, since she has up till now insisted that the child must be free, that the teacher must not intervene in the child's conduct. So she hastens to add that the teacher should *avoid the arrest of spontaneous movements*, movements that are useful. The teacher should suppress and destroy only the useless and dangerous acts.

Now, most teachers can fairly well spot dangerous acts, but what are *useless* acts? Montessori explains that useful acts are those that tend "to help toward the complete unfolding of this life."[37] The implication here is that useless acts do not so tend. But her teachers found it difficult to apply such a vague criterion—even the intelligent ones had trouble, she admits. As a result, many teachers became too indulgent. "When the teachers were weary of my observations," she complained, "they began to allow children to do whatever they pleased. I saw children with their feet on the tables, or with their fingers in their noses, and no intervention was made to correct them." Maria Montessori, however, soon set everyone right. She intervened and curtailed such behavior with "absolute rigor." This was necessary, she explained, so that "the child may come to discern clearly between good and evil."[38]

But this is a spurious explanation. For surely if the adult teachers could not discern good from evil, then clearly her intervention could not have conveyed such understanding to the young pupils. It is more likely that what the pupils did learn from such intervention was that Maria Montessori, or the directress, was the moral authority in the classroom, the authority for what is good and what is bad. Montessori tacitly admits this moral authoritarianism when she explains how the teacher can move the children on to collective discipline, or group cohesion. The teacher does this by arranging the children in order, by sending each one to his own place. As she does this, the teacher must try "to make them understand the idea that, thus placed in order, they looked well, and that it is a *good* thing to be placed in order, that it is a *good and pleasing arrangement in the room*; this ordered and tranquil adjustment of theirs."[39]

As Montessori herself decribes it, this collective order in the classroom emerges as a truly awesome obedience to the teacher: "If the teacher wishes the whole assembly to do something, for instance, leave the work which interests them so much, all she need do is to speak a word in a low tone, or make a gesture, and they are all attention, they look toward her with eagerness, anxious to know how to obey. Many visitors have seen the teacher write orders on the blackboard, which were obeyed joyously by the children."[40]

In *The Absorbent Mind*, Montessori cites what can only be called an eerie example of the total obedience the children displayed in one Montessori classroom. A directress of ten years' experience once reported to Montessori that one day she said to her pupils, "Put everything away before you go home tonight." The children did not wait for her to finish the sentence, but directly they heard her say, "Put everything away," they started to do it with great care and speed. They were caught up short when they heard the rest of the sentence, "when you go home tonight." Montessori cautions us that this teacher should have said, "Before you go home tonight, put everything away."[41]

How can one explain such amazing obedience? It is not that the teacher dispenses rewards or punishments—the Montessori classroom has no truck with rewards or punishments. Montessori herself claims that such obedience depends upon "a sort of miracle, occurring in the inner life of each child."[42] A more reasonable explanation would be that such obedience springs from the fact that the teacher in the Montessori classroom so successfully establishes herself as the *moral* authority.

The teacher has liberated the children: she has initiated them into an environment where they can be active creators who seek order. She facilitates their quest for order by helping them discover and eliminate what is wrong or mistaken in their present knowledge. She helps them to grow. Not unexpectedly, the children are grateful to the teacher. They love the teacher for what she has done for them. Therefore, they want to please her. They can see that none of the mistakes or errors that they make in the sensory-motor or cognitive exercises displeases the teacher, but they see that their mistakes in "moral" matters do displease her. Hence, they modify their conduct in light of her displeasure. Bad and disruptive students are never punished. They are isolated from the other students and given toys to play with. Tellingly, Montessori says that when a child is put into isolation he is made the object of special care, "almost as if he were ill." He observes the other children busily working, and little by little he gets better, he is cured of his bad behavior.

If I am correct in my understanding of Montessori's approach to moral and social education, then here she does contradict the theory inherent in her approach to intellectual education. In her moral and social education, the teacher must make the pupils dependent on her. She must intervene and impose predetermined modes of conduct on the pupils. The teacher must become authoritarian.

The source of Montessori's moral and social authoritarianism is not hard to find. I place it in her unacknowledged adherence to Thomistic Aristotelianism. Whereas I have interpreted Montessori's approach to education as part of a Darwinian theory of education, this is not how she viewed her own work. As she saw it, her work was rooted in the philosophy of Aristotle and Thomas Aquinas. According to Thomas Aquinas and Aristotle there is a natural order of things. There is an order to the physical universe, an ecological order to living organisms, a mathematical order to numbers and figures, a logical order to propositions. Her belief in the existence of such natural orders led Montessori to create responsive environments. That is, *because* there is a natural physical order of things, you can make mistakes in sensory discrimination or in motor movements: if you contravene the natural order, it responds—it gives you critical feedback. The Montessori classroom incorporates this natural order of the physical universe into an educative environment where children receive immediate feedback without harm. Her educative environment also incorporated the "natural order" inherent in the domains of language, mathematics, and plant life.[43]

Montessori, following Aristotle and Aquinas, also believed that there was a natural social and moral order. But this natural moral order is not present in the same way the other "natural orders" are. One can contravene the moral or the social order *without* receiving critical feedback. This is evident in a group of young children, where they can pick their noses or be rude *without* receiving critical feedback. Consequently, Montessori insists that here the teacher must become the representative of the moral and social order. The teacher alone can serve as the source of critical feedback to the students, informing them what conduct is wrong and in what ways.

Such an approach to moral and social education is most effective when used on little children. The unfortunate consequence of such an approach, however, is that it curtails autonomy and inculcates dependency, a dependency upon some moral authority, an authority to be obeyed. Not unexpectedly, Montessori regarded obedience as the law of life: "How many people have had the deeply spiritual experience of

an ardent desire to obey something or some person leading them along
the path of life—more than this, a desire to sacrifice something for
the sake of this obedience."[44]

This "education for obedience" contravenes the ideal of the autonomous learner that Montessori so well worked out in the areas of intellectual growth. And it contravenes what I have called her Darwinian approach to education. To discover a Darwinian approach to moral
and social education, we must turn to the work of A. S. Neill of Summerhill.

6

A. S. NEILL

A. S. Neill (1883–1973) was among Montessori's harshest critics: "I see Montessori becoming a dead, apparatus-ridden system," he wrote. As he saw it, she overemphasized the intellect—at the expense of the aesthetic and the creative: "She is always a scientist, never an artist." At one point, he declared, "I rather fear that one day a grown-up Montessori child will prove conclusively that the feet of Maud did not, when they touched the meadows, leave the daisies rosy. No, the Montessori world is too scientific for me; it is too orderly, too didactic. The name didactic frightens me."[1]

Most of all, Neill scored Montessori for her moralistic approach to education. "Her religious attitude repels me. She is a churchwoman; she has a definite idea of right and wrong. Thus, and though she allows children freedom to choose their own occupations, she allows them no freedom to challenge adult morality."[2] Not that Neill opposed moral education. Far from it. He viewed moral education as far more important than education of the intellect, "a thousand times more important." What he objected to was the imposition of morals on the young, "character moulding," he called it. In this regard, he liked to quote Shaw's remark: "The vilest abortionist is the person who tries to mould a child's character."[3] For Neill, Maria Montessori was one of the character molders: she imposed a readymade code of morals on her children.

Neill spent his entire career working out a nonauthoritarian approach to moral education. As I interpret it, his approach is Darwinian. Here he is in concert with Montessori. For just as she is Darwinian insofar as she created an educative environment to facilitate the growth of sensory-motor skills, language acts, and arithmetical abilities, so Neill is also Darwinian insofar as he constructed an environment to facilitate the growth of social and moral conduct. Neill's school and Montessori's Children's Houses look like entirely different kinds of educational enterprises. Yet they both reveal a Darwinian conception of growth, a procedure of selection via trial-and-error elimimation. Like Montessori, Neill constructed an educative environment that is free, responsive, and supportive, wherein children can learn from their mistakes. He called it Summerhill.

A FREE SCHOOL

A. S. Neill founded Summerhill in 1921. Situated in Leicester, in Suffolk, England, it is a boarding school for children who range in age from five to sixteen. "When my wife and I first began the school," Neill wrote, "we had one main idea: *to make the school fit the child—* instead of making the child fit the school."[4] In place of authoritarianism there was freedom, freedom for children to be themselves.

Most people usually differentiate between "authority" and "authoritarian." Authority goes with an office or role: a parent is an authority; a teacher is an authority. Authoritarianism, however, refers to the manner or mode of exercising authority, that is, to exercise it in a manner that accepts no criticism, brooks no complaints: the authoritarian wields power with impunity. Neill realized that all children perceive all adult authorities as authoritarian. They regard a grownup authority, such as a parent or a teacher, as someone who can usually exercise his or her authority with impunity. What can a child do when confronted by a decision made by an adult? The child cannot usually criticize or complain. He must accept.

Because children view all adult authorities as authoritarian, Neill deliberately removed all authority in his school: "We had to renounce all discipline, all direction, all suggestion, all moral training, all religious instruction."[5] Instead of authoritarianism—real or perceived—

there was to be freedom. In Summerhill, children were to be free to be themselves.

Summerhill students are free to dress as they please, maintain their rooms as they wish, talk as they like—to curse, or swear, or use dirty language—free to smoke, chew gum, eat candy, masturbate.[6] The newspapers call it a "do as you please school," a gathering of wild primitives. Neill called it a free school. "I believe," he wrote, "that to impose anything by authority is wrong. The child should not do anything until he comes to the opinion—his own opinion—that it should be done."[7]

In Summerhill, adults do not tell children how to behave, what to think, how to feel, what to say. Neill was the headmaster, but he was no authority. To the children, he was "Neill"—someone to tell when they broke a window but not someone who would punish or lecture them. Neill removed all of the traditional authority that accrues to a headmaster, retaining only the "natural" authority of an adult. And even this he dissipated by his jokes and pranks and general demeanor in his interactions with the children.

Once I asked a boy of fourteen to come and have a chat with me. He had just come to Summerhill from a typical private school. I noticed that his fingers were yellow with nicotine, so I took out my pack of cigarettes and offered it to him. "Thanks," he stammered, "but I don't smoke sir."

"Take one, you damned liar," I said with a smile and he took one. . . .

He had been expelled from his private school for stealing. "I hear you are a bit of a crook," I said. "What's the best way of swindling the railway company?"

"I never tried to swindle it, sir."

"Oh," I said, "that won't do. You must have a try. I know lots of ways," and I told him a few. He gaped.[8]

Neill's rejection of authoritarian education was not simply the rebellion of an iconoclast. True, he *was* an iconoclast—long before he established Summerhill. But his commitment to a nonauthoritarian education was deep rooted. It sprang, first of all, from his acceptance of human fallibility. "No man," he insisted, "is good enough to tell another how to live. No man is wise enough to guide another's footsteps."[9] Second, his nonauthoritarian approach to education emerged from his theory of human growth. He believed that human growth can occur only in an environment of freedom. Children do not need to be forced to grow. They need only freedom. In a free environment, they will grow—naturally.

The free environment of Summerhill does not extend to activities that endanger the life or well-being of the children. Neill did not ask a six-year-old to decide whether or not he should go outdoors when he was running a temperature. Nor did he ask a rundown child whether or not he should go to bed when he was overtired. Neill prohibited children from climbing roofs, and he banished air guns and other weapons that might wound. In addition, children could go swimming only when there was one lifeguard present for every six children, and no child under eleven could cycle on the streets alone.

The last two rules came from the children themselves, voted in a General School Meeting. The General School Meeting set forth the rules and laws that regulated the activities of the school. The General School Meeting was the "authority" at Summerhill. But this combined legislative and judicial body did not curtail the freedom of the children. It enhanced it: simply because all the children participated in the making of the laws that governed social life at Summerhill.

Everything connected with social or group life, including punishment for social offenses, was settled by a vote at the Saturday night General School Meeting. Each member of the teaching staff and each child, regardless of age, had a vote. There was a different chairman at each meeting appointed by the previous chairman.

Anyone who had a grievance, or charge, or suggestion, or new law to propose brought it up. Neill related how he once brought forward the notion that swearing be abolished by law. The reason he gave was that the parent of a prospective student was shocked by the swearing of the students and, as a result, refused to send her son to Summerhill. "Why should my income suffer because some fathead swears in front of a prospective parent?" he asked. A boy of fourteen answered: "Neill is talking rot. Obviously, if this woman was shocked, she didn't believe in Summerhill. Even if she had enrolled her boy, the first time he came home saying damn or hell, she would have taken him out of here." Neill reports that the meeting agreed with the boy. The proposal to abolish swearing was voted down.[10]

Neill stressed the educational value of the General School Meeting. "In my opinion," he wrote, "our weekly General School Meeting is of more value than a week's curriculum of school subjects."

And what about school subjects?

Since Summerhill was a school, it had to have lessons, but since it was a free school, all lessons were voluntary. Neill insisted that a school that makes active children sit at desks studying mostly useless subjects is a bad school. At Summerhill, children could go to lessons or stay away from them—for years, if they wished. Usually, children attended classes according to their age, but sometimes according to their interest.

How did children handle this freedom to go to class or stay away? Those who came to Summerhill as kindergartners learned lessons from the beginning of their stay; but students from other schools usually stayed away for a time, often a long time. One girl reportedly stayed away from lessons for three years. The average period of recovery from "lesson aversion" was three months.

And when they stayed away from lessons, what did they do? They played and cycled, Neill admitted, and generally got in people's way. But no one was ever compelled to attend class. (Of course, if a student came to English on Monday and did not make an appearance again until Friday of the following week, the others quite rightly objected that he was holding back the work, and they may have thrown him out for impeding progress.)

The practice of optional class attendance brought forth many criticisms of Summerhill: "The children will learn nothing." "They will be handicapped in competition with students from other schools." But these criticisms do not hold up. Neill reported that while most children did nothing but play most of the time, when it came time to take the government exams (Summerhill had no exams of its own) those who *wanted* to go to college sat down and set to work to master the subjects. They usually began at about fourteen, and in a little over two years a boy or girl covered the work that took children in normal schools eight years to cover.

As Neill saw it, books are the least important apparatus in the school. This is because he insisted that the learning side of school is unimportant. Intellectual growth will take care of itself, he counselled. Children, like adults, learn what they want to learn. "Young Freddie Beethoven and young Tommy Einstein will refuse to be kept away from their spheres." For Neill, the important side of education was the affective, the education of the emotions, by which he meant the growth of personality and character: moral and social education.

Most schools and most teachers try to do both: they take on the responsibility for both moral-social and intellectual education. But from Neill's angle of vision, intellectual education is always impositional. Giving lessons is always an authoritarian activity. Here he was wrong. Fr as we saw in the last chapter, the Montessori approach to intellectual education was nonauthoritarian (although her version of moral and social education *was* authoritarian). Nevertheless, since Neill could see no way to provide nonauthoritarian intellectual education, he made intellectual education voluntary, relegating it to a low priority in his eductional scheme.

In Summerhill, the child was allowed to do as he pleased only in things that affected *him*, and only him. "He can play all day if he wants to because work and study are matters that concern him alone. But he is not allowed to play a cornet in the school room because his playing would interfere with others."[11]

Neill continually cautioned against excessive freedom, labeling it "license," which he defined as interfering with another's freedom. Children who enjoy license become spoiled, as illustrated by the following anecdote:

Once a woman brought her girl of seven to me. "Mr. Neill," she said, "I have read every line you have written, and even before Daphne was born, I had decided to bring her up exactly along your lines."

I glanced at Daphne who was standing on my grand piano with her heavy shoes on. She made a leap for the sofa and nearly went through the springs. "You see how natural she is," said the mother, "The Neillian child!" I fear that I blushed.[12]

Freedom, Neill said, over and over, does not mean spoiling the child. "If a baby of three wants to walk over the dining room table, you simply tell him he must not."

The difference between freedom and license was embodied in the basic principle of the school: "Each individual is free to do what he likes, as long as he is not trespassing on the freedom of others."[13] This principle assured that Summerhill was a responsive environment as well as a free one.

A RESPONSIVE ENVIRONMENT

A responsive environment, as we saw in the case of the Montessori approach, is an environment that provides students with critical feedback, an environment that reveals their mistakes. As I viewed the Montessori classroom, the principle agenda was intellectual growth. The responsive environment, therefore, consisted of didactic materials and equipment that supplied critical feedback to the students' sensory, motor, linguistic, and mathematical skills. But at Summerhill, the agenda was social and moral growth. So here the responsive environment consisted of critical feedback from other people to the students' actual social and moral conduct.

Summerhill was a community. What made it a community was its basic principle: do not trespass on the freedom of others. Whenever somebody—be he a student, a teacher, the cook, or the headmaster— acted in a way that adversely affected somebody else in Summerhill, then the person adversely affected responded: he complained, or criticized, or in some way let the offender know that his actions hurt another.

Through living in this responsive community, children discovered the actual consequences of their actions. Others in the community provided critical feedback to their conduct: they pointed out mistakes, identified errors. (Mistakes and errors are actions that hurt or harm others.)

One day, Neill tells us, a boy borrowed his best saw. The next day, he found it lying in the rain. Neill told him he would not lend him that saw again. This was a critical response to the boy's conduct. The child had to learn that one cannot borrow someone else's tools and spoil them. "To let a child have his own way," Neill concludes, "or do what he wants to do *at another's expense*, is bad for the child. It creates a spoiled child, and the spoiled child is a bad citizen."

Another incident involving a bully dramatically demonstrates how Neill tried to create a responsive environment:

One day, on entering the playroom, I found the children all clustered together at one end of the room. At the other end stood the little terror with a hammer in his hand. He was threatening to hit anyone who approached him.

"Cut it out, my boy," I said sharply. "We aren't afraid of you."

He dropped the hammer and rushed at me. He bit and kicked me.

"Every time you hit or bite me," I said quietly, "I'll hit you back." And I did. Very soon, he gave up the contest and rushed from the room.

This was not punishment. It was a necessary lesson: learning that one cannot go about hurting others for his own gratification.[14]

Neill was not the only source of critical feedback. Children also receive feedback from one another. When a bòy mocked a new pupil who was lame, the other children called a special meeting and the offender was told by the community—and in no uncertain terms—that the school did not relish bad manners.[15] Most of the critical feedback from students came out at the General School Meetings. Here anyone could voice complaints and criticisms of the conduct of others. At the meeting, the assembly decided upon the appropriate punishment. Punishments were nearly always fines: hand over pocket money for a week, or miss a movie; sometimes the punishment was especially designed for the offense:

> Three small girls were disturbing the sleep of others
> Punishment: they must go to bed an hour earlier every night for a week
>
> Two boys were accused of throwing clods at other boys
> Punishment: they must cart clods to level the hockey field
>
> When the secretary was tried for riding Ginger's bike without permission, he and two other members of the staff who had also ridden it were ordered to push each other on Ginger's bike ten times around the front lawn.[16]

In the responsive environment of Summerhill, the child became what Neill calls self-regulating. As I understand self-regulation, it means that the child can modify or change his conduct in light of its recognized inadequacies or mistakes. There was no moral instruction at Summerhill; no one told a child how to behave. But children did improve their conduct. They learned from their mistakes.

Self-regulation does not happen straight off. It usally took a newcomer a while to become self-regulating. For in order to become self-regulating, one must become self-critical. And this takes time. A self-critical person accepts his fallibility, and he is open to criticism. He recognizes the fact that he does make mistakes, recognizes that he does act in ways (not always by design) that hurt others. He is on the lookout for the consequences of his actions that do adversely affect others, and he is open to critical feedback from others about his actions. Once a child becomes self-critical—once he accepts his fallibility and becomes open to criticism—he can modify or change his conduct in light of its unwanted and unexpected consequences: he becomes self-regulating.

But even before a child can become self-critical, he must acquire self-distance. He must separate his actions from his self. It is true that a person's actions disclose his personality and character, but *he* is not his actions: he can act differently. His actions are freely chosen. He can do this rather than that.

Children cannot readily distance themselves from their actions. Consequently, they take any criticism of their conduct as a criticism of themselves: they "take it personally." (This is true of many adults as well.) They cannot distinguish between a moral judgment, which condemns the act ("That is stealing and stealing is bad!") and moralizing, which condemns the person ("That is stealing and you are bad!"). Children, therefore, perceive all moral judgments of their conduct as instances of moralizing, as condemnations or rejections of themselves. It is for this reason that Neill renounced all moral instruction at Summerhill. "I believe that it is moral instruction that makes the child bad. I find that when I smash the moral instruction a bad boy has received, he becomes a good boy."[17]

What happened, of course, when Neill "smashed" the moral instruction a child had received was that the child was freed from adult authority telling him what to do. He was on his own to learn from his mistakes. But in order to learn from his mistakes he had to become self-critical, and this happened only after he acquired self-distance: he had to be able to separate his own self from his actions.

The most important way that Summerhillians developed self-distance was through play. Neill gave a Reichian explanation of the role of play at Summerhill, identifying play as a way that children "worked through" their complexes and frustrations and problems. Yet it is just as reasonable, I think, to interpret play as a low-pressure situation that provides children the security to try out (disclose and enact) their personalities and characters.[18] In play, the child presents his self through various actions and conduct. These actions, as all actions, have consequences. Whether he is engaged in solitary or group play, these actions receive critical feedback: for example, the response reveals that he throws the ball too slowly, or to the wrong person, or too late, or too far, and so forth. But because he is "just playing," because he knows it is "only a game," he realizes that his mistake is no "big deal."

In the low-pressure context of play, the child can come to recognize that his actions have consequences—some that adversely affect others. Second, in this low-pressure, secure, context he can come to accept the responsibility for those consequences. And finally, the child, in this context, learns how to eliminate his errors, learns how to learn from his mistakes. He discovers that *he* is not his actions, he can do this rather than that, he can modify his actions—and he does (he throws the ball better). Through play, the child acquires that self-distancing necessary to become self-critical. He accepts his fallibility, he becomes open to critical feedback, and he begins to modify his conduct in light of criticism.

When the child becomes self-critical, he acquires the power to be self-regulating, to modify or change his conduct in light of the harmful effects it has for others. At this point we can say that the child has learned how to improve his moral and social conduct. The child has become morally and socially sensitive—sensitive to the consequences of his actions. But in addition to becoming self-regulating, that is to say, self-critical, the Summerhill student also learned how to protect himself: he learned to become critical of others when their actions adversely affected him.

The moral and social education that went on at Summerhill differs from the traditional moral and social eduction given in most schools, including the Montessori school. The traditional approach makes moral and social education a matter of transmission, called socialization. The teacher imposes on the students those predetermined modes of conduct and patterns of behavior that will help the child to "adjust to" or "fit in" the present society.

Some critics have taken Neill to be a "socializer," too, socializing children to "fit in" at Summerhill. This kind of socialization, the critics say, does not prepare students to live in the outside ("real") world. But Neill was not in the socialization business. He said, remember, that the main idea of Summerhill was to fit the school to the child, not the child to the school. He explicitly rejected socialization and replaced it with a notion of a self-regulating community. Through the General School Meetings, the school adapts to the existing student body. There existed no predetermined "Summerhillian" set of behaviors or modes of conduct that had to be imposed on all students. The Summerhill community itself changed and modified its rules and mores and cultures as the student body itself changed. This happens, of course, at all schools, but at Summerhill the changes were conscious, deliberate, and freely taken. The General Meeting was a communal procedure of deliberate trial-and-error elimination.

The agenda of each General School Meeting consisted of concrete issues that explored the significance and the varied applications of the basic principle, "each individual is free to do what he likes, so long as he is not trespassing on the freedom of others." Some samples of these concrete problems of individual freedom in a community appear in Herb Smitzer's *Living at Summerhill*, where he reproduced verbatim reports of the meetings. Here are some of the problems discussed: problems of noise before breakfast, at supper time, during times when some people are listening to records; problems of leaving the school grounds; problems of leaving on the lights; problems with boys urinating on the toilet seats.[19]

By dealing with the concrete issues of human conduct that arise each week, the community learned how to apply the main principle, how to interpret it, how to formulate specific extensions of the rule, and how to amend these extensions. The community learned how to be self-regulating, and it learned this by making mistakes—as a community. At one weekly meeting, a new regulation would be proposed, discussed, and passed. In time, all came to recognize that it was in some way inadequate. So in time, at another general meeting, the community modified, changed, or repealed the regulation. Just as individuals do, the community grew or improved through the selection procedure of trial-and-error elimination.

We can see then that Summerhill was not without rules, regulations, limits. The differences between Summerhill and other schools, however, was that at Summerhill students participated in making—and changing—the rules and regulations. Children participated in this simply because all laws existed to protect members of the community. But because laws are created by fallible human beings, they are not always adequate. So at Summerhill students learned that the laws could be improved, via criticism.

Participation in this self-regulating community developed social responsibility, a particular kind of social responsibility, one that is laced with tolerance: an outlook of "live and let live." At Summerhill, the children learned that the preservation of a free community is the responsibility of its memebers. They had to see to it that the community was both open and responsive: open to criticisms of existing policies, laws, practices, procedures; open to complaints; open to cries of pain. And responsive to all criticisms, complaints, and cries of pain. This openness and responsiveness always existed at Summerhill. It needed only to be maintained. And although Neill himself did not harbor too much hope for the larger society, he did sometimes indicate that Summerhill's graduates might take on responsibility for improving society itself, making it more open and responsive. "Summerhill aims at a new democracy of free citizens who will not follow any leader. Until children are no longer moulded into castrated sheep, democracy remains a fake and a danger."[20]

Social responsibility at Summerhill included a readiness to intervene in the lives of others. Not to do good for them, but to protect them from harm, or perhaps better: to help them to protect themselves. No Summerhillian told another what is good, or how he should behave, or what he should do. Every Summerhillian believed that everybody should be free to pursue happiness in their own ways. The interventionism that happened at Summerhill—to help others when they are suffering, when they are hurt, when they are in pain—preserved the freedom and dignity of others. And to create and maintain such freedom for all it was necessary to tend to those arrangements that helped people to protect themselves. This is what students at Summerhill learned to do through participating in the General School Meetings.

The moral and social sensitivity that children developed at Summerhill allowed them, when they left, to live in any society or any social group. The Summerhillian is self-regulating, which means that he can learn from his mistakes. He is ready and able to change and modify his conduct through trial-and-error elimination: he will eliminate those actions that do adversely affect others. Moreover, the social responsibility the child developed from participating in the self-regulating Summerhill community well prepared the graduate to work to improve the existing arrangements in the larger society, such as changing the larger society to allow people more freedom. This does not mean that graduates of Summerhill entered politics. Few did. "If one of my old pupils became Prime Minister," Neill wrote, "I would feel that Summerhill had failed him."[21] But old pupils can and do improve society by working to create more open and responsive arrangements in their families, in their work, in their social activities. In a follow-up study of fifty ex-Summerhill students, Emmanuel Bernstein discovered that almost all had created free and responsive environments in most aspects of their lives.[22]

I have attempted to explain the moral and social growth of children in Summerhill as an instance of Darwinian evolution: growth takes place through the selective procedure of trial-and-error elimination. In the free and responsive environment of Summerhill, students can learn from their mistakes. Yet the willingness to change, refine, and modify one's conduct in the light of critical feedback does not come easily or readily. Nor could it ever come if Summerhill—in addition to being a free environment and a responsive environment—were not also a supportive environment.

A SUPPORTIVE ENVIRONMENT

The success of Summerhill, according to Neill, was due to the following commandment: Thou shalt be on the child's side. Being on the side of the child is giving love to the child; not possessive love, not sentimental love, just behaving toward the child in such a way that the child feels you love him and approve of him. Although Neill originally tried to provide therapy to the students at Summerhill, he eventually discovered that his territory was prophylaxis, not therapy.

He spent years analyzing the dreams of children who came to Summerhill and was proud of the fact that those chucked out of other schools for stealing or lying or being delinquent graduated from his school cured. But then he discovered that other boys and girls who had refused to come to him for analysis *also* left Summerhill cured. It was freedom and approval that had cured them.

He concluded that his chief job was to sit still and approve the conduct of the child: "A new boy swears. I smile and say, 'Carry on! Nothing bad about swearing.' So with masturbation, lying, stealing, and other socially condemned activities."[23]

Neill's commandment, "Thou shalt be on the child's side," generates skeptical questions like: What would you do if a boy started to hammer nails into the grand piano? His answer is, it doesn't matter what you do if your attitude is right. As long as there is no moralizing and nothing that the child can construe as moralizing, you can insist on individual rights. If the child realizes that you are on his side, you can even swear at him when he does things that adversely affect you.

Neill was quite willing to admit that there is a perennial conflict between the individual and the community, and when freedom becomes license he does not condone the conduct. In this regard, he related the reaction of a visiting psychologist to a General School Meeting where a girl was criticized: "It's all wrong. The girl's face is an unhappy one; she has never been loved, and all this open criticism makes her feel more unloved than ever. She needs love, not opposition."

"My dear woman," Neill replied, "we *have* tried to change her with love. For weeks, we rewarded her for being antisocial. We have shown her affection and tolerance, but she has not reacted. Rather, she has looked on us as simpletons, easy marks for her aggression. We cannot sacrifice the entire community to the individual."[24]

When, however, it was a matter of freedom, not license—when, that is, the "bad" or "naughty" acts did not trespass on the freedom of others in the community—then Neill unhesitatingly was on the side of the child. He reported that the cure of more than one thief began when "I joined him stealing our neighbor's hens or helped him to rob the school's pocket money drawer."[25]

Why does approval work? Why does it cure children? Neill said that the child needs love. When he is loved, the child's natural goodness emerges. Summerhill, the approving environment of Summerhill, releases what is hidden, or submerged. All this sounds like romantic twaddle that most people take with a grain of salt, if they don't reject it outright. Yet I think Neill is correct. The child does need love, and when he feels loved, he improves his moral and social conduct. A supportive environment is necessary—essential—to moral and social growth, which takes place, as we saw, through a Darwinian procedure of trial-and-error elimination. Without a supportive environment, the procedure does not lead to growth.

When the child feels support, or approval, he can "take criticism" and can modify his conduct in light of it—in light of the pain or harm it causes others. If, however, the child does not feel loved, he perceives all criticism as a rejection of himself. When the child feels rejected, criticism does not lead him to improve his conduct. He fails to react to criticism and modifies his conduct only when it has consequences that adversely affect himself.

Most "normal" children, however, do have "normal" parents, who do express love and support for their children—*when they behave correctly*. With parents—and teachers—like this, children can and do react to critical feedback by modifying or changing their behavior to more or less conform to the parents' dictates. But here the support provided by the parents and teachers is contingent upon proper conduct, and such support can be withdrawn at any time. So the "normal" child often harbors fears and anxiety—and resentment—most of which he hides most of the time.

As for problem children, Neill said that there are no problem children, only problem parents. This sounds foolish on first hearing, yet Neill is correct. So-called problem children are created by parents who fail to provide children with a supportive environment. Problem parents are those who rarely—or inconsistently, or never—support their children. When this happens, most children react in a common sense way: they become indifferent. Neill reported that many a "problem" girl has said to him: "I can't do a thing to please Mommy. She can do everything better than I can, and she flies into a temper if I make a mistake in sewing or knitting."[26] If nothing a child does wins support or approval from adults, then it makes no difference whether he does this or that. The child becomes uncaring, indifferent to the consequences of his acts—and thus ceases to react "normally" to critical feedback: he does not modify or change his conduct in light of criticism. He becomes a "problem child."

When children are care-less, when they are indifferent to the consequences of their actions, when they fail to react to critical feedback, parents and teachers (again, common-sensically) punish them. The effect of the punishment is to convert a problem child's indifference to hatred. For now, the child construes the punishment inflicted by the parent or teacher as an act of hatred, and he usually reacts by hating the parent or teacher in return. (Or he may react by hating himself and feeling guilty.) If the child cannot disclose the hatred directly—or symbolically, via acts of destruction or cruelty—he may withdraw and create a fantasy world of his own, a world where he is not the object of hatred.

Problem children came to Summerhill in droves. They left as happy, responsible children. The haters, the destroyers, the withdrawn—Summerhill cured them all. The chief ingredients of the curing process were "the showing of approval, of trust, of understanding." In his long career, Neill dealt with many problem children, many of them delinquents. These unhappy and hateful children were arrogant and disrespectful to him because he was an authority, the enemy. He lived with their hatred and suspicion. But in a few short years at Summerhill, these same haters went out into the world as happy, social beings. "So far as I know," Neill wrote, "not one delinquent who spent seven years in Summerhill was ever sent to prison, or ever raped, or ever became anti-social. It was the environment that cured them—for the environment of Summerhill gives out trust, security, sympathy, lack of blame, absence of judgment."[27]

Love and approval will not cure a case of acute claustrophobia or a case of marked sadism, Neill admits, but generally, love will cure most thieves and liars and delinquents. His work at Summerhill proved this. Take thieving. Neill cured this by rewards. No matter what a child stole—money, tobacco, food, toys, whatever—Neill responded by rewarding him or her. Almost all young thieves reacted well to these rewards. They stopped stealing. The reason for this is that the rewards made the child realize that Neill approved of him. Even if he consciously thought Neill was a fool for rewarding him, the young thief realized that Neill was "on his side." Neill also used rewards with bedwetters. Here, too, the reward was a symbolic expression of approval; it told the child that it is all right to wet the bed. And in time, these children stopped.

Neill's resolve to be on the child's side sometimes made him lie in order to demonstrate his approval of the child. One time, a girl who had an unhappy history stole a pound. The theft committee of the school, three boys, saw her spend money on ice cream and cigarettes, and they cross-examined her. "I got the pound from Neill," she told them, and they brought her to me, asking, "Did you give Liz a quid?" Hastily sizing up the situation, Neill replied blandly, "Why, yes, I did." Had I given her away, Neill explained, she would have never had trust in me. . . . I had to prove that I was on her side all the way."[28]

If love and approval (and freedom) help to cure problem children who come to Summerhill, then what happens with "normal" children?

When "normal" children first come to Summerhill, Neill reported they went through a period of antisocial conduct. These seemingly normal children, as I noted above, harbored feelings of fear and anxiety about the possible withdrawal of adult love and approval. So when they came to see that approval freely given by Neill and other adults at Summerhill was *not* contingent upon any predetermined "correct" conduct, they gave vent to their suppressed fears and anxieties—and resentment—in antisocial behaviors. This soon disappeared and they became self-regulating.

Neill cited the case of a seventeen-year-old boy who came to Summerhill from a private school. A week after his arrival, he became

chummy with the men who filled coal carts at the station, and he began to help them with their loading. His face and hands were black
when he came to meals. No one said a word. No one cared. After
several weeks, he gave up coal heaving and once more became clean
in person and dress, but with a difference: he wanted to be clean.

Why does approval work?

Why do children who feel that they are loved react to criticism by
modifying or eliminating the conduct criticized? Neill explained this
by claiming that the child is naturally good.[29] So when the child lives
in a free and supportive environment, this natural goodness emerges.
I do not think children are naturally good, but they can always become better. And this, I think, is to be explained in Darwinian terms.

The child is an active creator who seeks order—social order as well
as cognitive order. And he seeks order in a negative way: by a selection procedure of trial-and-error elimination. That is, he tries out
conduct and then modifies it in light of its recognized inadequacies:
he learns from his mistakes. Those acts that create disorder are mistaken or inadequate. In a responsive environment, the child gets critical feedback to those acts, or to the consequences of those acts, that
adversely affect others. So in a community the child's antisocial acts
create disorder. And when the environment is supportive, as well as
responsive, then the child does eliminate his bad conduct: he modifies
that conduct that causes disorder.

But why? Why does a supportive environment do this?

We can say that a supportive environment allows the procedure of
trial-and-error elimination to function "correctly." That is, in a supportive environment, the child discovers that the love and approval
given to him is *not* contingent upon his conduct, is *not* contingent
upon his elimination of his offensive behavior. Therefore, he eliminates his offensive behavior. This sounds paradoxical, but perhaps a
comparison of what happens at Summerhill with what happens in a
"normal" home, or in a "normal" school, can clear it up.

In a "normal" home or school, the adults make their support for the
child contingent upon the child's "correct" conduct. The child always
seeks order, which, in the social realm, for all young children, means
to seek to avoid pain and hurt *to himself.* So in the "normal" home or
school, the child modifies his conduct more or less in accord with the
demands of the adults. The child conforms. Yet the child perceives
this adult love as something that can be withdrawn at any time.

Therefore, he not only harbors resentment toward these adults, he is also wholly self-centered, self-concerned. He is worried about getting and holding on to the love and support of his parents or teachers. Thus, when a "normal" child comes to Summerhill, where love and approval are freely given, where it is not contingent upon "correct" behavior, then the child gives vent to the rage caused him by his fears, anxieties, and resentment about the love withheld from him before. But more important than this brief explosion of antisocial conduct is the fact that in this unconditional supportive environment the child is now freed from his quest for love and approval. He can and does become less self-centered. He can begin to become concerned with the welfare of others.

This is a matter of becoming a member of a community. As long as the child is uncertain about the love and approval adults provide, he will remain self-absorbed, self-centered. This is how he seeks order, or better, how he seeks to escape from disorder. Disorder for him, is *his own* personal pain and hurts. This is what he seeks to avoid or escape. But when a child experiences unconditional support, he becomes less self-absorbed, less self-centered. He becomes a member of the community and concerned about community disorder. When a child becomes a member of a community, however, he recognizes that other people also suffer pain and hurt, sometimes as the result of *his* conduct, and he begins to understand that this creates community disorder. As a member of the community, he seeks order for the community by trying to eliminate whatever creates disorder.

Becoming a member of the Summerhill community was facilitated by the fact that Summerhill was such a responsive environment. In Summerhill, the child could not escape from critical feedback. At Summerhill, he was forced to recognize that the community existed, forced to become sensitive to the pain others felt. Neill says that because Summerhill was a self-governing community, "each one is constantly being compelled to see the other person's point of view."[30] In such a responsive environment, which was at the same time a supportive environment, the child in time began to react to criticism by modifying his behavior. He became self-regulating. He improved his moral and social conduct. His character and personality improved.

Now this did not happen quickly. It took time. Moreover, Neill sometimes shielded the child from all critical feedback until the child was certain he was loved, secure in the adult support provided him.

Only then could the child take criticism. "If I should be painting a door and Robert came along and threw mud on my fresh paint," Neill says, "I would swear at him heartily because he has been one of us for a long time and what I say to him does not matter. But suppose Robert had just come from a hateful school and his mudslinging was an attempt to fight authority, I would join with him in his mudslinging because his salvation is more important than the door. I know that I must stay on his side while he lives out his hate in order for him to become social again. It isn't easy. I have stood by and seen a boy treat my precious lathe badly. I know that if I protested he would at once identify me with his stern father who always threatened to beat him if he touched his tools."[31]

Neill's long experience with children helped him to know when a child was ready for criticism, when not.

Bill, a new boy, has stolen some money from another child. The victim asks me, "Should I charge him in our next General Meeting?"

Without thinking, I say, "No, leave it to me." I can reason it out later. Bill is new to freedom, uneasy in his new environment. He has been trying so hard to make himself popular and accepted by his fellows that he has been swaggering and showing off a great deal. To make his theft public would be to give him shame, fear, followed perhaps by defensive and an outbreak of anti-social behavior. . . .

Another time, a child says, "I am going to charge Mary for stealing my crayons," and I am not interested. I do not consciously think of it at the time, but I know that Mary has been in the school for two years and can handle the situation.[32]

Approval must come first. The child must feel loved, must feel supported. He must feel free to be himself. Then, in time, he will be able to take criticism.

With problem children, the curing took longer. They came from an environment that they perceived as one of hatred. Their self-absorption was deeper and more pronounced since they believed that their quest for order—that is, their elimination of disorder, which is to say, their escape from hatred—depended solely on themselves, on their aggression, or their withdrawal, or their cunning. In time, however, Summerhill cured them. They became self-regulating. They improved their social and moral conduct.

It is important to repeat that the moral and social education in Summerhill did *not* consist of a set of behaviors that was imposed upon children. Education in Summerhill was not socialization. Summerhill simply allowed the child to engage in trial-and-error elimination in a broader context—the context of a community—instead of being focused solely on himself. The free, responsive, and supportive environment of Summerhill facilitated the development of the child's sensitivity to the adverse consequences that his acts have for others, and it facilitated his readiness to react to critical feedback by modifying his conduct when it offended others. This sensitivity and this readiness allowed the child to continue to improve—for the rest of his life. For as with intellectual growth, social and moral growth is endless.

RESERVATIONS

As I understand it, Summerhill promoted social and moral growth. But Neill had a cavalier disregard for intellectual growth. I would even say he was irresponsible. ("Young Freddie Beethoven and young Tommy Einstein will refuse to be kept away from their spheres.") This irresponsibility actually sprang from his concern with moral and social growth. For Neill knew, correctly, that authoritarianism would undermine such an engagement. So he made Summerhill a nonauthoritarian school. There had to be academic lessons, of course. But Neill thought, incorrectly, that one could not promote intellectual growth without being authoritarian. So he made academic lessons voluntary, claiming that children would learn what they needed, when they needed it.

The invalidity of this romantic claim is found in the fact that the one widely shared complaint that graduates expressed to Bernstein about Summerhill was the lack of emphasis on intellectual growth. For children do not learn naturally, voluntarily. Children, like all of us, seek order. So we learn only when we discover that our present knowledge is inadequate, when we experience cognitive disorder. And this, as Montessori realized, is the task of the school: to create cognitive disorder, to reveal to students the inadequacy of their present knowledge. If students are not challenged, disequilibrated, they will not grow.

I recommend that teachers adopt the approaches of both Montessori and Neill, the one for promoting intellectual growth, the other for promoting moral and social growth. They can do this because both are Darwinian. Both embody the metatheory of learning from our mistakes. Both have the teacher creating educative environments—free, responsive, supportive environments wherein students can grow.

Few schools are like Summerhill, which was probably the freest, most directly responsive, and most supportive school in the world. Yet few public schools could be like Summerhill, if only because Summerhill was a private boarding school. What Summerhill does is hold out an ideal for public day schools to be guided by. Every teacher can make his or her classroom a *more* free, a *more* responsive, a *more* supportive classroom than it is now.

7

CARL ROGERS

Like both Maria Montessori and A. S. Neill, Carl Rogers (1902–   )
has a theory of education that can be interpreted as Darwinian. Like
them, Rogers rejects the authoritarian notion that the teacher transmits knowledge and instead, like them, views the teacher as a creator
of educative environments. For him, too, an educative environment
is free, responsive, and supportive, an environment where nonauthoritarian education takes place, an environment where students can learn
from their mistakes.

As I interpreted the Montessori method, it is a Darwinian approach
to intellectual growth; as for Neill's Summerhill, I found it to be a
Darwinian approach to social and moral growth. With Carl Rogers,
the agenda is psychological growth. Psychological growth, like intellectual and moral growth, is Darwinian: it takes place through the selection procedure of trial-and-error elimination. Just as people "try out"
knowledge and conduct and then eliminate the errors and mistakes
contained therein, so they also "try out" their "selves" and then eliminate the errors and mistakes they discovered in the selves they have
constructed. These errors or mistakes in the constructed self cause fears,
anxieties, and hang-ups. Psychological growth consists of the elimi-

nation or diminution of these anxieties, fears, and hang-ups about one's self.

Rogers, like Neill, has tried to insist that his agenda is *the* agenda for education. The goal of education, he claims, is "the fully functioning person," which is also the goal of therapy. It is not likely, however, that education will become therapy, nor teachers therapists. Yet helping young people to feel better about themselves, helping them to grow psychologically, does seem to be one of the functions of the teacher in the twentieth century, in addition to the functions of facilitation of intellectual growth and social and moral growth.[1]

Rogers's original work was in the field of psychotherapy, where he created an approach to therapy that he only later applied to teaching. So before discussing how a teacher can facilitate psychological growth in a classroom, we should examine Rogers's approach to psychotherapy.

CLIENT-CENTERED THERAPY

Rogers has a nondirective approach to therapy—he calls it client-centered therapy. This approach repudiates the traditional notion that the therapist knows best, denies that *he* can diagnose a client's problems, rejects the notion that *he* can tell the client how to solve the problem. As Rogers sees it, the traditional approach construes the client as a passive receptor who needs to be controlled and directed. In contrast, Rogers's theory sees the client as capable of self-direction. Here is how he puts it: "The individual has a sufficient capacity to deal constructively with all the aspects of his life which can potentially come into conscious awareness."[2] Rogers calls this *the* hypothesis of the client-centered therapist.

Underlying this hypothesis is Rogers's acceptance of the belief that human beings tend toward self-enhancement or self-actualization. "The therapeutic process," Rogers has written, "is, in its totality, the achievement by the individual, in a favorable psychological climate, of further stages in a direction which has already been set by his growth and maturational development from the time of conception onward."[3] This belief that under the proper conditions human beings tend toward self-enhancement is a metaphysical belief: there are no possible conditions that could falsify it. Even if it were true, it does not provide any news about psychological growth. It tells us nothing about how growth takes place. Be that as it may, Rogers shares this metaphysicsal belief in the nature of human nature with other romantic theorists like Neill and Rousseau. Yet there is no need for this questionable assumption about human nature, since it is possible to explain psychological growth as an instance of Darwinian selection. A Darwinian interpretation of psychological growth does explain why client-centered therapy works, whereas the assumption that human beings tend toward self-enhancement explains nothing.

The Darwinian conception of human beings, as we saw in part I, is that we are active creators who seek order. We human beings create knowledge, and we create our conduct. In the matter of intellectual growth, the quest for order leads us to avoid, or overcome contradictions. In the matter of social and moral growth, the quest for order leads us to avoid or eliminate the pain or suffering caused by our conduct. In the matter of psychological growth, we create our own selves, or more precisely, we create a self-concept, or a theory of self. And we seek order here by trying to overcome the contradictions to our self-theory.

According to Rogers, a person's self-concept, or theory, consists of three kinds of perceptions, or subtheories: subtheories or perceptions of the characteristics of the "I" or "me"; subtheories or perceptions of the "I" or "me" in relation to others; and subtheories or perceptions of the values attached to those two perceptions. For example, a perception of the "I" or "me" might be: "I am five feet in height." A perception of the "I" in relation to others might be: "I am short." The value attached to these perceptions might be: "I am too short."

A person's theory of his self consists of a collection of organized subtheories. Some of the subtheories may be false but still may be effective. As long as he does not recognize their falsity, he may have positive self-feelings and view his self as worthy and acceptable. His behavior will be consistent with his self-theory, and he may perceive it as adequate. For example, the star student in a small-town high school may perceive himself as an outstandingly brilliant person. This theory might serve him well as long as he remains in that environment.

Problems arise when a person's behavior becomes inconsistent with his theory of self, or when he perceives discrepancies within his theory of self, or when his self no longer functions adequately in the reality situation. As examples of these three kinds of problems, Rogers mentions the client who perceives that his behavior is unpredictable, "not like myself," or no longer understandable; the client who wants to marry the girl, yet does not want to; and the "brilliant" small-town high school student who finds himself not effective in the university.[4]

In each of these three kinds of problems, the person experiences a contradiction to his self-theory: his own behavior contradicts his self-theory, or his self-theory contains internal contradictions, or events in the real world contradict his self-theory. These problems can be serious enough for him to seek therapy. Through therapy—client-centered therapy—the client overcomes these contradictions and reduces his anxieties, fears, hang-ups.

Client-centered therapy, unlike directive therapy, casts the therapist into the role of facilitator. The therapist poses no questions, undertakes no analyses, issues no directions. Here is how one client described his experience in client-centered therapy: "Much to my surprise, Mr. L., the counsellor, let me talk myself dry, so to speak. I thought he might question me on various points of my problem. He did to a small extent, but not as much as I had anticipated. In conferring with Mr. L., I listened to myself while talking. And in doing so, I would say that I solved my own problems."[5]

In client-centered therapy, the therapist merely "clarifies" or, better, "reflects" what the client says; he reflects the "objective content" of what the client says. He refrains totally from questions, comments, or reflections that delve beyond the statements the client makes. This nondirective approach does facilitate growth. Here is part of an exchange between Ernest (E) and his therapist, Virginia Axline, (T), one of Rogers's students when he was at Ohio State University. Six-year-old Ernest was very insecure and unable for psychological reasons to take food orally. He had to be fed intravenously, not able even to swallow water without regurgitating it. When this discussion takes place, Ernest and his therapist are in school watching the other children gleefully drinking from the water fountain.

E. It looks like fun.

T. You think it would be fun to drink from it too?

E. (Nods agreement.) But I can't.

T. You don't think you could drink it?

E. It looks like fun.

T. You don't think you could drink it, but still you would like to?

E. I'd like to try.

T. You want to try it?

E. I used to take a drink from one of those things when I was in the hospital, but I don't drink now.

T. You remember what fun it was? (E. grins and goes over to the drinking fountain.)

E. It might not stay down.

T. You think it might not stay down, but you still want to try? (E. nods his head. He takes the handle and turns it up too high and jumps back.)

E. It's a lot of water.

T. It looks like a lot of water to you.

E. I'll drown myself. (He takes a drink, glances at the teacher, grins broadly.) It stayed down.

T. Yes, it stayed down.

E. (Drinks again.) It stayed down. (He seems quite delighted.)[6]

Rogers has identified three phases in client-centered therapy: 1. release; 2. insight; and 3. positive action based on insight.

In the first phase of therapy, release, the client unburdens his problems and concerns, he discloses his feelings and attitudes: he bares his self. The therapist has no special techniques for evoking this release from the client. What is all important, however, is the attitude of the therapist: he must be accepting. He neither approves nor disapproves of what the client tells about his self, he simply accepts and respects the client as he is.

This means that there are no *conditions* for acceptance; acceptance is not contingent upon the client doing this or saying that. And it involves acceptance of the client's "bad," painful, defensive, normal feelings as well as his "good," positive, mature, confident feelings. It means acceptance of the attitudes the client now has and continuing acceptance of his attitudes, whether they become expressions of despair, plaints of confusion, or declarations of confidence. It means that the therapist prizes the client as a person of worth. Rogers has sometimes expressed all this by saying that the therapist must have "unconditional positive regard" for the client.

The therapist's attitude of complete acceptance creates a free environment for the client. In this climate of freedom, the client can freely disclose all his feelings and attitudes; moreover, he is free to explore them and free to choose, to select what he will try to eliminate, what he will retain. This freedom must be thorough and complete if therapy is to succeed. Some idea of how thoroughgoing this freedom should be comes out in these questions Rogers poses:

Is the therapist willing to give the client full freedom as to outcome? Is he genuinely willing for the client to organize and direct his life? Is he willing for him to choose goals that are social or antisocial, moral or immoral? . . . Is he willing for the client to choose regressing rather than growth or maturity? To choose neuroticism rather than mental health? To choose to reject help rather than accept it? To choose death rather than life?

Rogers's own answer is that it is "only as the therapist is completely willing that *any* outcome, any direction may be chosen—only then does he realize the vital strength of the capacity and potentiality of the individual for constructive action."[7]

In the second phase of therapy, insight, the client begins to make connections between his feelings and the events he relates to. He begins to see relationships of cause and effect, begins to see patterns in his conduct, begins to understand the significance of his actions.

What he perceives is that his present self-concept, or self-theory, is false, or mistaken, or inadequate in some way. It is necessary that the client himself make this discovery; the therapist merely facilitates. By reflecting the objective content of what the client tells him, the therapist provides the client with critical feedback. By this technique of reflection, the therapist objectifies or makes concrete the client's own feelings and attitudes. This "objective content" of what he himself has said becomes critical feedback to the client. ("You think it might not stay down, but you still want to try?") The critical feedback helps the client to recognize and experience what he had previously denied or distorted, the contradictions inherent in his theory of self; or he begins to see that his theory of self is insufficient to account for what he really is; or he begins to see that his theory of self is simply false.

In addition to the critical feedback, which consists of the objective content of what the client tells the therapist, Rogers, in his later work, insists upon another kind of feedback to the client—feedback from the therapist himself. The therapist, Rogers says, must be real, or congruent. By this he means that the therapist must be a unified person, "with his experienced feelings, his awareness of his feelings, and his expression of these feelings all congruent or similar."[8] Thus, if the therapist is persistently bored in the interview or feels a persistent disbelief in what the client is saying, he should express these feelings and not pretend to be interested or believing. On first blush, this attitude of realness would seem to contradict Rogers's insistence that the therapist should be accepting, but in reality it is not. The therapist does not say to the client, "You are boring," or "You are lying." What he does is to express his own feelings. "I feel bored by this interview," or "I find myself disbelieving what you say." Such a statement about his real or genuine feelings does not affront or dismay the client. The client is not being rejected or contradicted.

By being real or congruent, the therapist provides the client with critical feedback from a real person, but in a way and in a context that does not threaten or frighten. The critical feedback helps the client recognize the actual impact that his presented self has on another "real" person. Once again, critical feedback helps the client to recognize that his theory of self is inadequate, contradictory, or simply false.

At this point, the client begins to see that his theory of self needs modification if he is to function adequately. This brings us to the third stage of client-centered therapy: positive action based on insight. A small, scared boy takes a drink of water from a water fountain. A man brings flowers to his sick wife whom he has resented. A mother changes her way of disciplining her son. These are self-initiated acts that begin the procedure of the self-modifications that begin to overcome the problems that afflict the client.

And the therapist? What is his role in this third phase? He does not make any suggestions, nor does he point out the possible consequences of proposed actions, nor does he even ask clarifying questions to help the client think through his situation. The therapist remains nondirective. But he does facilitate positive action by creating a supportive environment.

The therapist can facilitate positive actions by his attitude toward the client. For in addition to being accepting and real, or congruent, the therapist must express empathic understanding of the client, or of the client's internal frame of reference. This means that the therapist must be willing and able to understand the client's thoughts, feelings, and struggles from the client's point of view. The therapist's attempt to adopt the client's frame of reference must be done in a tentative and accepting manner—with empathy: seeing the world *as if* one were the client, but never so totally identifying with the client that the "as if" quality is lost.

This ability to look at what the client says from his internal frame of reference is difficult. Rogers provided the following excerpt of an interview to illustrate some of the difficulties:

Client: I don't feel very normal, but I want to feel that way. . . . I thought I'd have something to talk about—then it all goes around in circles. I was trying to think what I was going to say. Then coming here, it doesn't work out. . . . I tell you, I just can't make a decision; I don't know what I want. I've tried to reason this thing out logically—tried to figure out which things are important to me. I thought that there are maybe two things a man might do; he might get married and raise a family. But if he was just a bachelor, just making a living—that isn't very good. I find myself and my thoughts getting back to the days when I was a kid and I cry very easily. The dam would break through. I've been in the army four and a half years. I had no problems then, no hopes, no wishes. My only thought was to get out when peace would come. My problems, now that I'm out, are as ever. I tell you they go back to a long time before I was in the Army. . . . I love children. When I was in the Philippines—I tell you when I was young I swore I'd never forget my unhappy childhood—so when I saw these children in the Philippines, I treated them very nicely. I used to give them ice cream cones and movies. It was just a period—I'd reverted back—and that awakened some emotions in me I thought I had long buried. (*A pause. He seems very near tears.*)

What can a therapist say to this? He can make evaluative comments, judging what the client says from his own frame of reference:

I wonder if I should help him get started talking?
Is this inability to get under way a type of dependence?
Why this indecisiveness? What could be its cause?
What is meant by this focus on marriage and family?
He seems to be a bachelor. I hadn't known that.
The crying, the "dam," sounded as though there must be a great deal of repression.
He is a veteran. Could he have been a psychiatric case?
I feel sorry for anybody who spent four and one half years in the service.
Sometime we will probably need to dig into those early unhappy experiences.
What is this interest in children? Identification? Homosexuality?

These comments are all supportive, but the locus of perceiving is outside the client. In contrast, a client-centered therapist who was successful in assessing the client's internal frame of reference would make comments like:

> You're wanting to struggle toward normality, aren't you?
> It's really hard for you to get started.
> Decision making just seems impossible to you.
> You want marriage, but it doesn't seem to you to be much of a possibility.
> You feel yourself brimming over with childish feelings.
> To you the army represented stagnation.
> Being very nice to children somehow had meaning for you.
> But it has been—and is—a disturbing experience for you.[19]

In 1957, Rogers published an essay entitled "The Necessary and Sufficient Conditions of the Therapeutic Personality Change." In it, he claimed that when the therapist had the attitudes of acceptance, empathic understanding, and congruence—which create, as we have seen, an environment that is free, supportive, and responsive—then, over a period of time, constructive personality change will follow. Rogers spells this out: the client becomes more realistic in his self-percep-tions, more confident and self-directing, more positively valued by himself, less likely to repress elements of his experience, more mature, socialized, and adaptive in his behavior, more like the healthy, inte-grated, well-functioning person in his personality structure.

STUDENT-CENTERED EDUCATION

In his 1951 book, *Client-Centered Therapy*, Rogers included a chap-ter on "Student-Centered Teaching." If we can rely upon the capacity of the client to deal constructively with his life situation, he asked, then why not in education? Having rejected therapist-centered ther-apy because it was too authoritarian, Rogers now suggested that we replace teacher-centered education with student-centered education for the same reason. Not only is teacher-centered education authoritar-ian, it is based upon a false conception of education, the notion that education is a process of transmission. But this conception is wrong, Rogers insists, for "we cannot teach another person directly; we can only facilitate his learning."[10] Like the therapist, the teacher is to be-come a facilitator.

This suggestion that the teacher become a facilitator is more than simply a change of title, as Rogers made clear a year later at a now famous conference at the Harvard Business School. At that Conference, Rogers said:

It seems to me that anything that can be taught to another is relatively inconsequential, and has little or no significant influence on behavior. . . . I have come to feel that the only learning which significantly influences behavior is self-discovered, self-appropriated learning. . . . Such self-discovered learning, truth that has been personally appropriated and assimilated in experience, cannot be directly communicated to another. . . . As a consequence of the above, I realize that I have lost interest in being a teacher.[11]

What Rogers meant, of course, was that he had lost interest in being a transmission teacher. Henceforth, the teacher was to try to facilitate but not transmit. But if the task is to facilitate learning, then how does the teacher do this? It is the teacher's attitudes, Rogers explains. When the teacher is: real or congruent; accepting, prizing, trusting; and understanding, then significant learning takes place. In his 1969 book, *Freedom to Learn*, Rogers presents abundant evidence to demonstrate that his student-centered approach works. He reprinted a number of letters from students of Dr. Patricia Bull of Cortland College (New York), who had used the Rogersian approach in her class on adolescent psychology. Here is one such testimonial:

I appreciate the respect and concern you have for others, including myself. . . . As a result of my experience in class, plus the influence of my readings, I seriously believe that the student-centered teaching method does provide an ideal framework for learning; not just for the accumulation of facts, but more important, for learning about ourselves in relation to others. . . . When I think back to my shallow awareness in September compared to the depth of my insights now, I know that this course has offered me a learning experience of great value which I couldn't have acquired in any other way.[12]

According to Rogers, the classroom climate that the teacher creates facilitates learning of a different quality, proceeding at a different pace, with a greater degree of permanence. Feelings—positive, negative, confused—become a part of the classroom experience. Learning, Rogers concludes, becomes life, "and a very vital life at that." In this kind of classroom, the student is set on his way, sometimes excitedly, sometimes reluctantly, to becoming a learning, changing being. The students themselves become more real, more accepting, and more understanding.

A Rogersian approach does promote students' psychological growth. In his 1983 edition of *Freedom to Learn*, Rogers presents evidence from a study involving six hundred teachers and ten thousand students that shows that students of teachers trained to be real, accepting, and empathic had increased scores on self-concept measures, indicating more positive self-regard.[13]

In addition to psychological growth, a Rogersian approach also promotes intellectual and social growth. The same study cited above found that students of high facilitative teachers: made greater gains on academic achievement measures, including both math and reading scores; increased their scores on IQ tests (grades K–5); made gains in creativity scores from September to May; and were more spontaneous and used higher levels of thinking.

Rogers also relates the experience of Barbara Shiel, who used the student-centered approach with her sixth-grade class. She reported the following outcomes:

I continued the program until the end of the term, two months past the last report. In that time, there was a continuing change in these children. They still argued and fought among themselves but seemed to develop some regard for our social structure: school, adults, teachers, property, etc. And as they began to better understand themselves, their own reactions—the outbursts and quarrels—diminished.

. . . They developed values, attitudes, standards of behavior on their own, and lived up to those standards. They did not become "angels" by any means, but there was a definite change. Other teachers and playground supervisors seldom had to discipline them and commented on the change in behavior and attitude. They were rarely in the office for infractions and there was not one parental complaint the balance of the year! There was a tremendous change in parental attitude as the children evidenced success and growth, both academic and social.

I have neglected to mention the students who were not problems and those who were above average academically. I firmly believe that the gifted children were the ones who benefitted most from this program. They developed a keen sense of competition between one another, interest in mutual projects, and they sailed ahead, not restricted by the slow learners. Their achievement was amazing to me.

I found that the children who had the most difficulty learning also made great progress. Some who had been unable to retain the multiplication tables (which should have been learned in fourth grade) were able to multiply and divide fractions with a minimum number of errors by June![14]

Rogers also reports a study made by Volney Faw of Lewis and Clark College (Oregon) of the number and kind of "productions" completed by students taught with a student-centered approach. Faw compared this with the number and kinds of productions completed by students taught with a traditional teacher-centered approach. Not only did the student-centered group have a greater number and a greater variety of productions, their productions were more original and less stereotypical.[15]

With student-centered education, students learn more, improve their conduct and feel better about themselves. There is intellectual growth, social and moral growth, and psychological growth.

Why does student-centered teaching work? Why does it promote growth? My interpretation—already apparent from my analysis of client-

Number and Kind of Productions in Operant and Respondent Groups

	Teacher-Centered Respondent Group N 38	Student-Centered Operant Group N 38
Statement of goals	0	26
Journal articles reported	0	165
Research proposals	0	25
Experiments (original)	0	18
Group projects	0	3
Demonstrations	0	2
Library studies (term papers)	38	8
Field trips	0	23
Vocational test batteries	5	7
Counseling	0	1
HDI program	0	19
Interview with instructor	0	32
Other activities	0	4
Course examinations	190	190
Total productions	233	523
Mean	6.1	13.7

centered therapy—is that when the teacher is real, accepting, and understanding, these attitudes help to create an educative environment: an environment that is free, supportive, and responsive.

When teachers are accepting, they take seriously what a student says and does and feels; they treat their students with respect, with positive regard. In this interpersonal climate, students feel free to disclose their present knowledge, ideas, feelings, conduct.

Second, when teachers are real, or congruent, when they respond to what students say and do—respond honestly and directly, pointing out when they agree and when they disagree—this creates a responsive environment wherein the student receives critical feedback from a real person.

Finally, when teachers are empathic, when they try to see matters from the student's point of view, when they try to understand the student's ideas—not evaluate or judge them—this creates an environment that is supportive for the students.

In such an environment, human beings are free to disclose their present knowledge, conduct, and feelings; in such an environment, they receive feedback that helps them to recognize their mistakes and inadequacies; and in such an environment, they feel secure enough to eliminate their errors and try out new theories, new actions, new behavior. In short, student-centered education facilitates the selection procedure of trial-and-error elimination, the procedure through which all growth occurs—intellectual growth, social growth, and psychological growth.

ROGERS'S AUTHORITARIANISM

In my treatment of the educational approach of Carl Rogers—as with Montessori and Neill—I have accepted the fact that Rogersian teaching works — as does the Montessori approach, and as does Summerhill. But I have attempted to explain the success of Rogers's student-centered education by means of a Darwinian theory of education.

Yet Rogers, Montessori, and Neill did not give a Darwinian interpretation to their approaches to education. As a result, each approach is clearly limited and blatantly inadequate as a comprehensive approach to education. Montessori's transmission approach to moral and social education was authoritarian and promoted submission and obedience rather than autonomy and growth. Neill's approach to intellectual education—making it voluntary—was cavalier and irresponsible.

By providing a Darwinian interpretation of both Montessori's approach to intellectual education and Neill's approach to moral and social education, I have suggested that these can be combined into a comprehensive approach to education. With Rogers, we acquire an additional function for teachers: the concern for psychological growth. I have shown how Rogers's student-centered approach can be interpreted as Darwinian and thus be incorporated with approaches of Montessori and Neill.

But Rogers's student-centered approach to education includes a dimension I have not yet discussed: his conception of the curriculum, his notion of what is worth knowing. Here Rogers's theory becomes authoritarian.

Educational theorists have, in the past, taken two different approaches to the question, What's worth knowing? One approach, going back to Plato, starts with the society, either the existing society or, as in Plato's *Republic*, some ideal society. Accordingly then, the knowledge of most worth is that knowledge that is essential to the preservation of the society. The second approach, going back to Aristotle, takes its cues from the human being: the knowledge of most worth is that knowledge that will best help a human being realize his humanity.

These approaches are authoritarian insofar as both impose on students some predetermined knowledge. Rogers recognized this authoritarianism. "I wonder if in this modern world we are justified in the presumption that we are wise about the future and the young are foolish. Are we really sure as to what they should know?" He tells us that *he* is sure that the physics that is taught to the present-day students will be outdated in a decade—because, you see, we live in an environment that is continually changing. He goes on in this vein. The teaching of psychology will certainly be out of date in twenty years; the facts of history depend upon the mood and temper of the culture; and chemistry, biology, genetics, and sociology are in such flux that a firm statement made today "will almost certainly be modified by the time the student gets around to using the knowledge."[16]

So, how should we approach the question, What's worth knowing? Rogers would have the students themselves decide. Teachers should grant students freedom to learn—freedom to learn whatever they want to learn. Rogers recognizes that in most classrooms and schools there will be institutional constraints on the amount of freedom that teachers can extend to students. Yet teachers can, he suggests, work within those existing limitations and give students as much freedom as possible to choose what they determine is worth knowing.

Rogers presents three arguments for this approach to the question. First, he claims that this will lead to significant learning. By significant learning he means learning that will "change behavior." He argues that *only* learning that is self-initiated and meaningful to the learner, learning in which the learner is personally involved, only this kind of learning *will* change behavior.[17]

But there are numerous counter-examples to Rogers's argument. Few of us initiated learning how to read or write, or calculate, and these activities often seemed meaningless to many of us, but most of us have learned how: our behavior changed, the learning was significant, even though we did not freely choose to learn these skills.

Rogers's second argument for allowing students to choose what is worth knowing is that all human beings possess "an organismic wisdom" for deciding what is best or correct for each of us. So if a person is given the freedom to learn whatever he wishes to learn, he will choose those learnings that enhance his own development. Unfortunately, Rogers adds, most people—including students—have lost touch with their own organismic wisdom by taking over the conceptions of others about what is good, what is right. These introjected values divorce the person from his organismic wisdom.

By giving students freedom to choose what is worth knowing, each one will begin to accept his own self as the authority for what is right, what is good. In Rogers's words, "He would do what 'felt right' in the immediate moment and he would find this in general to be a competent and trustworthy guide to his behavior."[18]

Rogers admits that there is no guarantee that the choice made through "organismic wisdom" will, in fact, prove to be good, right, or self-actualizing. But, he argues,

Because whatever evidence exists is availabale to the individual and because he is open to his experiencing, errors are correctable. If this chosen course of action is not self-enhancing, this will be sensed and he can make an adjustment or revision. He thrives on maximum feedback interchange, and thus, like the gyroscopic compass on a ship, continually corrects his course toward his true goal of self-fulfillment.[19]

This is a specious argument. If someone made an error in choosing what is self-actualizing, why should he trust that his "corrections," or any subsequent corrections, will be without error?

Human beings are fallible. We cannot know the future; we do not know what is self-actualizing, what is not. Nor do we have any criteria we can rely on, any authorities we can turn to—internal or external—by which we can decide what will be right or good.

Rogers rightly recognized that all attempts to impose predetermined knowledge on students is authoritarian. But his approach to the question, What knowledge is of most worth? is authoritarian, too. By assuming that students have "organismic wisdom," he replaces the authoritarianism of the teacher with the authoritarianism of the student. We might call it psychological authoritarianism: the student's real interests will direct him to what is worth knowing.

But Rogers did not have to assume that human beings have organismic wisdom in order to explain why teachers (and therapists) promote growth when they are accepting, real, and empathic—any more than Neill had to assume that human beings are naturally good in order to explain why freedom and love promoted social and moral growth at Summerhill. Both Rogers and Neill, I have argued, created educative environments, environments that were free, responsive, and supportive. And because human beings are fallible creators who seek order, such an environment facilitates growth: in such an environment students can and do engage in the continual procedure of trial-and-error elimination, through which they improve their knowledge and their conduct, and their self-knowledge, too.

Rogers's third argument for giving students the freedom to decide what is worth knowing is that this is how they will learn how to learn. By focusing on his own interests, his own aims, his own problems, each student will learn how to learn.

Here Rogers does not present an argument as much as he asserts an assumption: "human beings have a natural potentiality for learning." By this he means that people are born curious, "eager to develop and learn."[20] But all learning, he adds, is painful, either painful in itself or painful because it involves giving up certain previous learnings. The trick, then, Rogers concludes, is for teachers to reduce or diminish the pain so that the student's potentialities for learning can actualize themselves. Students learn with facility when they perceive the subject matter has relevance for their own purposes, when the subject matter is not threatening, when it is something in which they are personally involved. Therefore, teachers should not impose learning on students, nor should they evaluate what students have learned. Students should be free to learn.[21]

Rogers is surely correct in pointing out that learning involves pain. But just as surely we cannot facilitate learning by allowing students to avoid or circumvent pain, which happens when they can choose what they will learn. Instead of assuming that human beings are naturally curious and will learn when the threat of pain is reduced, the theory I have proposed in this book rests on the assumption that human beings, like all organisms, seek order. To facilitate learning, or growth, students must receive critical feedback that helps them to uncover disorder in their present knowledge or understandings. This is painful, but necessary, if students are ever to improve their present knowledge.

Subject matter is an integral part of an educative environment designed to promote intellectual growth. Subject matter is not transmitted to students, rather is presented to them as an agenda, and they are invited to encounter it critically. This critical encounter educes from the students their present knowledge and, at the same time, probes or tests that present knowledge, helping them to discover inadequacies or disorders therein. Thus the subject matter, when it is presented in an invitational mode, creates what I have called a free and responsive environment. And when the environment is also sufficiently supportive, these critical encounters with the subject matter lead students to modify or improve their present knowledge in light of its uncovered inadequacies.

But what knowledge is of most worth? What knowledge should the students critically encounter?

At different times, and different places, and in different situations, people have come up with different answers to this question. Moreover, the decisions made about what knowledge is of most worth are never perfect, always inadequate: no matter who decides, no matter how they decide. All decisions about what's worth knowing are human decisions, and human beings are fallible.

Yet there must be a course of study for students, so we must decide what it will be, even though our decisions will be imperfect. I suggest that we approach such decisions in the same way we have come to approach our political decisions in a democracy. We hope for the best but prepare for the worst. Whether it is selecting political leaders, or passing laws, or making judicial decisions—none of these is final and irrevocable. We recognize our human fallibility in all of these decisions and have prepared for the worst by seeing to it that our political decisions are open to criticism and can be modified in light of the criticism when the criticism holds up. Moreover, in the political realm we have institutionalized the procedures for doing this: a constitution stipulating limited powers, separation of the powers of government, checks and balances among the three branches of government, frequent elections, recall, impeachment, judicial review, appeal—to mention but some of them. What is important here is that those who are adversely affected by a political decision do have adequate means of securing redress. This includes access to the decision makers in order to voice a criticism, some guarantee of a response from them, and some hope for a change in the decision in light of the unrefuted criticism.

If we approach the question, What's worth knowing? as we approach our political questions, then our first concern will be to devise institutionalized arrangements that will enable us to easily and effectively change our subject matters and our courses of study. We might, for example, adopt "sundown" and "sunshine" policies with regard to all subjects and all courses of study: each subject and course of study will be taught for a designated period of years, then critically assessed by all affected by it, students, alumni, parents, employers, teachers, administrators, other educators.

Just as we try to improve our political decisions via critical discussion of previous decisions, so we can try to improve our choice of subject matter in the school. We can never answer the question, What's worth knowing? but we can, through critical discussion of the existing subject matter, come up with subject matter that is *more* worth knowing than what is presently offered in the schools.

PART IV

Learning from Our Mistakes

8

A DARWINIAN THEORY OF EDUCATION

Throughout Western history there have been three dominant metaphors in education: the metaphor of initiation, the metaphor of transmission, and the metaphor of growth. Each of these metaphors supplies different conceptions of the nature of the pupil, different conceptions of the role of the teacher, and different conceptions of the content of education.

The initiation metaphor first appeared in ancient Greece and dominated educational thought and practice until the nineteenth century. With the initiation metaphor, education is content-centered: the content of education is the most important element in the transaction between the teacher and the pupil. The content consists of the cultural heritage of Western civilization—the best that has been thought, said, and done. Here the teacher is a master of at least a part of the traditional culture, a mentor who initiates the pupil into that culture. And the pupil is a student, one who studies, and what he studies are the books that contain his cultural heritage, the classic books, the great books.

The second metaphor, the transmission metaphor, first appeared in the seventeenth century as the child of the so-called new philosophy. The new philosophers wanted to advance knowledge, not just traditional wisdom; and this, they argued, could be obtained from careful sense observation of the real world. When applied to educational theory, this new philosophy gave birth to the transmission metaphor.

The transmission metaphor created teacher-centered education. For here the teacher is the most important element in the transaction. He plans and prepares the content of education—orders it, sequences it, packages it. The teacher must also prepare the pupil—motivate him, control him. Finally, the teacher must transmit the content to the pupil: this is called instruction. The pupil now becomes a learner rather than a student. He learns the content of education; he does not study it except to learn it. A learner is a more or less passive receptor of knowledge. As for the content of education, the transmission metaphor converts it into subject matter, the latest and most certain knowledge, all sorted out and organized into fields, or disciplines, and courses of study.

The transmission metaphor of education led to an authoritarian construction of education: teachers control pupils and impose knowledge on them; they shape and mold their pupils' behavior. It was in reaction against this authoritarianism of the transmission metaphor of education that Rousseau, in the eighteenth century, first proposed the metaphor of education as a matter of growth. This latest metaphor creates a pupil-centered education. Now the child is no longer a blank slate awaiting the transmission of knowledge, no longer an empty bucket waiting to be filled with knowledge, no longer a ball of wax to be shaped to his teacher's wishes. No, now the child is a dynamic organism that develops and grows. And the teacher's role is one of promoting or facilitating that growth.

Unfortunately, Rousseau's conception of *how* the child grows was nothing more than speculative romanticism. Later, in the nineteenth century, John Dewey concocted a new version of the growth metaphor according to which human growth is a matter of experimentation. Human beings grow, Dewey said, by solving problems, and they solve problems by experimenting.

But Dewey's version of the growth metaphor is inadequate, too, on two counts. First, by casting experimentation as *the* method to solve problems, Dewey ends up with an authoritarian theory of education. Second, his version of the growth metaphor is actually only another rendition of education as a process of transmission: the experiments that he would have pupils engage in in school are such that students simply *rediscover* the knowledge that teachers want to transmit to them.

Although most practicing educators continue to subscribe to the transmission metaphor, it is the growth metaphor that prevails in educational theory. It inheres in the work of most twentieth-century educational theorists, especially Montessori, Piaget, Skinner, Rogers, and Neill. In this book I have argued that all these theorists share a common conception of human growth—a Darwinian conception. The main features of the two competing educational metaphors are summarized in the following table:

Conceptions of Education, the Teacher, the Subject Matter, and the Student

The Transmission Metaphor	The Growth Metaphor
Education is a process of transmission.	Education is a procedure of (Darwinian) growth: trial-and-error elimination; the continuous modification of existing knowledge.
The teacher prepares the student, prepares the subject matter, and transmits (instructs, matches) the subject to the student in the form of lessons that the student learns.	The teacher creates an educative environment—an environment that is free, responsive, and supportive—wherein the student can improve (modify) his present knowledge through trial-and-error elimination.
The subject matter is what is transmitted; that which the student learns.	The subject matter is an agenda that specifies what aspects of the students' present knowledge are to be improved. The subject matter evokes the students' present knowledge and tests it (reveals the inadequacies in that present knowledge).
The student is a learner, a more or less passive receptor who needs to be controlled and motivated.	The student is a fallible, active creator of knowledge who seeks order. When he discerns contradictions (errors, mistakes, inadequacies) in his present knowledge, he will modify that present knowledge.

According to Darwin, biological evolution takes place by means of natural selection. Organisms create progeny, which vary slightly from their parents. Nature then selects, or eliminates, those that are unfit. The fit ones survive and have progeny of their own, which again vary slightly from their parents and from among which, again, nature selects, or eliminates, the unfit. Over time, as a result of many changes, new species evolve. This growth or evolution of the species is a matter of biological trial-and-error elimination. Each generation of organisms creates new trial progeny, and nature eliminates the errors.

Up until now, the greatest obstacle to a Darwinian theory of education has been the widespread spell of what I have called the common sense theory of knowledge. According to this theory, knowledge consists of ideas in the mind, which we receive from the outside, and these ideas are rational only if we can justify them. Finally, according to this theory, our ideas grow through induction.

Karl Popper has revealed the contradictions that riddle this common sense theory of knowledge and has proposed to replace it with a Darwinian evolutionary epistemology. According to Popper's theory of knowledge, human beings create knowledge. This knowledge has an objective existence—it is part of what he calls world three. We can never justify knowledge, but we can criticize it. And this is how knowledge grows: through criticism. That is, when we discover what is wrong with present or existing knowledge, we try to eliminate the errors and thereby improve it. We accept tentatively knowledge that has withstood criticism. We can say that such knowledge is rational.

In this book, I have used Popper's evolutionary epistemology as the basis for constructing a Darwinian interpretation of some of the leading twentieth-century educational theorists.

I have not attempted empirical validation of the claims these theorists have made for their approach to education. I have taken their claims of success at face value and have concentrated instead on their theories, their explanations of why their approaches were successful. Much of the book, therefore, has been a criticism of the theories they have put forward.

With Dewey, I accepted his construction of education as growth but rejected his criterion for growth (that which leads to more growth), since this criterion leads to an infinite regress: with this criterion we can *never* establish that any change is an instance of growth. I also rejected his claim that the scientific method is the method of problem solving, since *the* scientific method is rather a method for raising problems (with any and all solutions). But I did accept his contention that growth begins with a problem, taking "problem" as a synonym for an inadequacy, an error, a mistake in our present knowledge.

With Piaget, I accepted his conception of the knower as a fallible creator who seeks order. I did not reject, but do not find it necessary to accept, the existence of cognitive structures. What is beyond doubt is the existence of an invariant order of cognitive development, but this may be the result of a necessary (logical) sequence of learning: first sensory-motor acts, then language acts, then concrete and formal operations.

With Skinner, I rejected both his determinism and his claim that learning takes place through operant conditioning. In place of this, I argued that all organisms learn from their mistakes, via the selection procedure of trial-and-error elimination. I accepted, however, his Darwinian notion that genetic endowment is the result of contingencies of survival (via trial-and-error elimination) and especially stressed that one such innate disposition of human beings is their aversion toward contradictions. I also accepted Skinner's notion that all advance in knowledge is simply the modification of existing knowledge. But I argued that the learner himself does this modifying, not the environment.

With Montessori, I rejected her approach to moral and social education as being authoritarian and actually inconsistent with her approach to autodidactic intellectual growth. The latter I accepted as the paradigm for the role of the teacher in promoting growth.

With Neill, I rejected as irresponsible his approach to the intellectual function of schooling but accepted his approach to social-moral growth as a matter of helping students to become self-regulating.

With Rogers, I accepted his approach to promoting psychological growth and accepted that such an approach facilitated intellectual and social-moral growth as well. But I rejected his conception of what is worth knowing as being romantic and authoritarian.

Here I want to bring together the various contributions of these several theorists to what I have called a Darwinian educational theory. This theory gives us a new conception of the pupil, a new conception of the role of subject matter in education, a new conception of the role of the teacher, and a new conception of the aim of education.

THE CONCEPTION OF THE PUPIL

According to the Darwinian interpretation I have presented, human beings create knowledge, and conduct, and their self-concepts, too. They create theories about the universe they inhabit, and they create skills to cope with that universe. Note that both Skinner and Piaget agree that human beings create knowledge. As I have interpreted these theorists, both construe human beings as active creators who seek order. Accordingly, then, human beings literally "make sense" of the world; they create their own understandings; they are the artificers of their own skills. Knowledge is not transmitted or transferred from one human being to another, nor is it transmitted by a book. It is not received nor discovered. Knowledge is created. Every knower is the creator of what he knows.

But note also that human beings are fallible, so that the knowledge they create is never perfect: their theories contain errors and mistakes; their skills prove inadequate. And their conduct is never perfect either. This means that the knowledge created by the child in the third grade is imperfect, and so is the knowledge created by the nuclear physicist. It means that the conduct of the holy man is imperfect, as is the conduct of the thief. And it means that the self-understanding of the psychoanalyst and that of the neurotic are both imperfect. We say, of course, that the nuclear physicist has better knowledge, the holy man better conduct, the psychoanalyst better understanding, but this means only that these people make fewer mistakes than the child in the third grade, the thief, the neurotic. All knowledge, all conduct, all self-understanding is conjectural—the conjectures of fallible human beings.

Yet although they are always conjectural, knowledge, conduct, and self-understandings can be improved, can become better, can progress and grow. All we create grows along the lines suggested by Darwinian theory, that is, through selection, through elimination of what is unfit, through elimination of what is false, mistaken, erroneous, inadequate, limited. This selection or elimination happens naturally, as it were, insofar as the knowledge, conduct, and self-understandings that we create do interact with the universe we inhabit. And that universe eliminates, or wipes out, whatever is unfit or mistaken.

We human beings, however, can ourselves act on our present knowledge, our present conduct, and our present self-understanding without waiting for nature to eliminate our mistakes. This is preferable because nature, when it eliminates errors, often eliminates us.

(Think of what nature does to us when we have erroneous knowledge about the depth of a pool of water into which we dive.) This critical elimination is possible, first of all, because we have language. This enables us to encode the knowledge we have created. And we can use language to describe our conduct and to describe our self-concepts. Thus, through language, we can convert our theories, our conduct, our self-understandings into objective knowledge. As objective knowledge, it can be criticized. Criticism is the procedure through which human beings discover contradictions in knowledge, in skills, in conduct. All organisms, as Piaget has shown, can discover contradictions, although we humans do this best after reaching the operational stage of cognitive development. With our theoretical knowledge, a contradiction inherent in a theory or a contradiction between one theory and another signals that something is wrong, that we have made an error. Likewise with our skills and our conduct: when these lead to unexpected consequences—when there is a contradiction between what we expect to happen and what actually happens—this tells us that our present skills or conduct are inadequate. In the matter of our conduct, contradictions take the form of pain. When we do not expect our conduct to cause pain—to ourselves or to others whom we care for—and discover that it does, then we know our conduct is wrong. Moreover, as we saw, human beings have a sense of order, which means that we always seek to avoid or overcome contradictions. Contradictions are *aversive* to us—to use Skinner's language; or human beings tend toward *equilibrium*—to use the language of Piaget.

Because contradictions are aversive to us, we try to overcome them, or eliminate them. One way to do this is to modify, change, or refine our knowledge: we alter our theories when they lead to contradictions; we revise our skills when they have results that contradict our expectations; we modify our conduct when it causes pain. This is the procedure of trial-and-error elimination. This is how we learn from our mistakes.

If this Darwinian theory of human growth is correct, then teachers should view pupils as fallible creators who seek order. Pupils do not receive knowledge; they do not have conduct imposed on them. Pupils create knowledge; they are the agents of their conduct. This means that they always come to classrooms and schools with knowledge. Whether they are entering kindergarten or graduate school, they arrive with theories, understandings, skills, patterns of conduct.

But pupils are not only creators, they are fallible creators. This means that pupils' existing understandings are wrong, their present skills in-adequate. The dumb ones and the smart ones, too. All are ignorant. Those in kindergarten, elementary school, high school, college, and graduate school. Indeed, this is why they have come to school: to dis-cover their ignorance, to find out their mistakes.

But more than this, they have come to school to improve their un-derstandings, skills, and knowledge. And the good news about human fallibility, the optimistic news, the exhilarating news, is that pupils can always improve their knowledge and conduct. All they need is a teacher who can help them discover where their present knowledge is inadequate.

For pupils are not only fallible creators of knowledge, they are also organisms that seek order. This is why the discovery of a mistake, an error, an inadequacy, leads to improvement. Pupils, like all human beings, have an aversity to mistakes, that is, to contradictions. So they try to overcome contradictions by eliminating the error. According to this interpretation, pupils learn, or improve, or grow, by modifying their present knowledge or present conduct. They modify it in light of the discovered errors, mistakes, and inadequacies it contains.

What this means is that pupils do not have to be motivated to learn, or compelled to pay attention, or controlled, or coerced. Pupils learn, that is, modify their present knowledge or conduct, when they dis-cover that it is inadequate. Note that it is the pupil *himself* who must recognize and admit the inadequacy, error, or mistake. It is not suffi-cient for someone else (like a teacher) to point it out. Pupils must discover their own errors.

Whether they are learning typing or history, physics or computer programming, Latin or arithmetic, pupils are always autodidacts: they learn on their own, by themselves, by discovering what is wrong with their present understandings, skills, and theories. They learn through the selection procedure of trial-and-error elimination.

Note that this theory does not assume that pupils are naturally good or wise, or that they are naturally curious, or even that they are nat-ural learners. Learning takes place if and only if the pupil encounters cognitive disequilibrium, if and only if the pupil recognizes that he has made an error. Once the pupil recognizes an error in his own knowl-edge or conduct, he eliminates it in a new trial. This new trial is an improvement insofar as the error was reduced or diminished. This is how pupils learn from their mistakes.

THE ROLE OF THE TEACHER

The teacher helps the pupil to learn from his mistakes by facilitating the selection procedure of trial-and-error elimination. The crucial point—as all twentieth-century educational theorists have insisted—is that the teacher must create an educative environment for the pupils. In an educative environment, students can recognize, or discover, the mistakes or errors in their present conduct or present knowledge, eliminate them, and try again. As I see it, an educative environment has three characteristics: it is free; it is responsive; and it is supportive.

A free environment allows, even provokes the student to disclose his present knowledge, his conduct, his self-concept. A responsive environment provides the student with critical feedback, which helps him to discover what is mistaken, inadequate, or insufficient in his present knowledge, conduct, or self-concept. And a supportive environment allows .the student to make a new trial in which the error is eliminated, the inadequacy overcome, the insufficiency abated. When the environment is free, responsive, and supportive, then growth—intellectual, social and moral, and psychological—all take place through the selection procedure of trial-and-error elimination.

In my Darwinian interpretation, the teacher is always pupil-centered. However, the teacher centers not on what the pupil *wants* to know but on what he already knows; not on how the pupil would *like* to act (or how the teacher would like him to act) but on how he *does* act; not on the self the pupil would *like* to be but on the self he *is*. The teacher's task is to help the pupil improve his present knowledge, conduct, and self-understanding.

Promoting Intellectual Growth

In the realm of intellectual growth, the teacher's task is to help the pupil to improve his present knowledge. So the initial step is to create an environment where the pupil feels free to disclose that knowledge. In a free environment, pupils are not ashamed of their present knowledge, nor are they afraid to reveal it, to make it public.

A free environment emerges, in part, from the teacher's attitudes. Teachers should accept and respect their pupils' present skills and understandings, neither judging, nor censuring, nor disdaining, nor dismissing them. Indeed, the teacher should prize the disclosures of the pupils' present knowledge, not because it is good or adequate but because it is the starting point for improvement. The teacher should try to express this trust that the pupils' present knowledge can get better, this trust that the pupils themselves can improve it.

In addition to the teacher's additudes toward the pupils' present knowledge, a free environment is also dependent upon the teacher's conception of subject matter content and his understanding of the role of the subject matter in the educational transaction.

A Darwinian teacher conceives subject matter as the imperfect creation of fallible human beings. Physicists create physics, historians create history, mathematicians mathematics, and so on. This includes skills, too: human beings created swimming, typing, singing, writing, dancing, painting. We have inherited a vast array of theories and skills created in the past. All of them are conjectural, but they have evolved and grown through time—via criticism. Those that still exist or still have currency are "rational," insofar as they are the ones that have withstood criticism. This "rational" knowledge constitutes the subject matter content.

What role does subject matter content play in the educational transaction?

The Darwinian teacher does not present the subject matter as the final word, or even as the best knowledge available. Rather, the teacher presents the subject matter for what it is: conjectural knowledge that can still be improved—via additional criticism. In short, the teacher presents the subject matter to the pupil as something to be criticized, something to be improved. Pupils are invited to criticize the subject matter content, not because it is unimportant and worthless but, indeed, precisely because it is important and full of worth. Our subject matter consists of answers to questions and solutions to problems that are of central concern to human beings in the present civilization. It is the importance of these answers and solutions that makes it worthwhile for us—the teacher can explain—to try to improve them via criticism.

When the subject matter content is presented in this invitational mode, it evokes pupils' present knowledge; it provokes them to disclose their own answers to the problems or questions addressed by the subject matter. Take physics, for example. This consists of conjectural answers to a number of specific questions about the universe. Now, pupils all have their own answers to those questions, although *their* answers are usually vague, inchoate, poorly articulated. Because of this, pupils are often reluctant to disclose their own theories. But if the teacher has demonstrated open, accepting, prizing, trusting attitudes toward the pupils' present knowledge and if the subject matter content is presented as conjectures of fallible human beings, then pupils will be more likely to disclose their own theories. They will do this in the very criticisms that they make of the theories the physics teacher presents to them. For, you see, their criticisms must come from their own present theories.

So the primary function of the subject matter content is to evoke pupils' present knowledge. Each subject matter, each "lesson," specifies an agenda, a problem area: history evokes the pupil's present knowledge about the past; physics, his theories about the universe.

There are various ways for the teacher to use the subject matter to this end. The teacher may simply present the material—by lecture, by readings, or video tapes—and then secure a critical reaction from the pupils either orally ("What do you think?") or in writing in the form of critical reaction papers. Or a teacher may employ both critical dialogues about the subject matter content and written critical reactions, thus permitting all students to disclose their present knowledge.

In the area of skills—reading, writing, typing, drawing, boxing, woodworking, and so forth—the teacher can demonstrate the skills and ask the pupils to imitate them. The pupils' trial efforts reveal their present levels of knowledge.

The teacher can also educe the pupils' present knowledge of skills through materials, examples, exercises, problems. In the lower grades, for example, teachers have available a wide variety of materials and apparatus that will educe the pupils' present manual, interpretative, and conceptual skills.

Note that with this conception of the subject matter and this understanding of the role of the subject matter content in the educational transaction, the teacher does not *transmit* knowledge to pupils. Throughout this book, I have argued that teachers cannot transmit knowledge because knowledge is created, not received. Pupils create their knowledge. Teachers can present knowledge to pupils, but pupils then create their understandings of what has been presented. But although transmission does not exist, there do exist teachers who try to transmit knowledge. This creates a coercive rather than a free environment. Students do not feel free to display their present skills when the teacher is hell-bent to transmit, or to impose, a set of predetermined skills or understandings on them.

It is important to note, however, that a free environment is not sufficient to facilitate the growth or improvement of knowledge. Having pupils make public their present knowledge may simply strengthen that knowledge or increase their commitment to it rather than lead them to improve it.

What I want to stress here is that a free environment will facilitate the improvement of knowledge *only* if it is at the same time a responsive environment. In a responsive environment, pupils receive critical feedback to the knowledge they have made public. They find out what is wrong, or mistaken, or inadequate in their present understandings or present skills.

The teacher's role here is to create a responsive environment to help the pupil discover his mistakes. As both Montessori and Skinner have made clear, a responsive environment is a structured environment. If a pupil encounters no structure when he discloses his knowledge or conduct, he will receive no critical feedback. Actually, the physical universe (what Popper calls world one) has a structure, as does the world that human beings have created, the world of culture, the world of artifacts, language, knowledge (what Popper calls world three).

The structure of the physical universe gives us critical feedback when we perform sensory or motor acts: we cannot put large-diameter pegs into small-diameter holes. So in the growth of our sensory-motor skills the physical environment itself is a responsive environment. As Montessori did, teachers can and do provide special materials that encode or embody the obdurate structure of the physical universe so that pupils can obtain responses in safe and exploratory procedures. In the case of advanced motor skills—like swimming, typing, carpentry, sewing, automobile mechanics—the structure of the physical environment *and* the structure of the man-made environment (typewriters, automobiles, hammers and nails, needles and thread) provide critical feedback to the pupils' trial efforts to do or make something.

In the area of language skills we can readily see that the world of language is also structured and, therefore, is a "natural" responsive environment that will provide critical feedback to the pupils' trial efforts at speaking, writing, reading. Language has a grammatical structure, a syntactical structure, and a structure of vocabulary such that every object, action, and event has its own name. Children learn language through interaction with this world of language, through interaction with those who speak, write, and read language. This takes place as the child receives critical feedback to his trial efforts to make utterances and to understand the utterances of others—as he tries to speak and listen, write and read. Teachers can and do facilitate this growth by creating environments wherein pupils receive regular and continual critical feedback to their utterances and to their trial understandings of the utterances of others.

In addition to the natural structure of the physical universe and the natural structure of language, there is a "logical" structure inherent in each and every subject matter field. In mathematics, this is obviously the case. But this is so of all other fields, too. In physics, for example, it is not possible to make any statement one wishes about the physical universe, that the moon is ten miles from the earth, for example. For there is a logical structure to our physics such that a statement like this can be shown to be false because it contradicts other statements that are part of that structured body of knowledge we call physics. Likewise with the subject matter of history: there is a logical structure inherent in this body of knowledge which excludes statements about the past that contradict it.

It is important to note that the structure of language changes over time, as do the structures of physics, history, and all subject matter areas. Moreover, most physical scientists now accept indeterminism, which says that the structures of the physical universe also change over time. But this does not mean that no structures exist—only that they change. In creating responsive environments, teachers who are trying to promote the growth of sensory skills, or motor skills, or some practical skills do construct and fashion lessons, units, exercises, and projects that encode or embody the natural structures that inhere in the physical universe and in the world of artifacts man has invented. Teachers employ the natural structures inherent in language when they try to promote the growth of language skills, and teachers employ the logical structures of the various subject matter fields when they try to promote growth in these areas. Teachers use these structures to construct a responsive environment that will provide critical feedback to the pupils' trial efforts to make, to do, to understand.

There are numerous ways a teacher might create responsive environments, depending in large part on the level of development of the pupils and the subject matter itself. With older pupils—those who can take criticism—the teacher serves as a critic, directly helping students to discover the errors and inadequacies of their present knowledge. With younger pupils and those who have difficulty in taking criticism, the teacher can use materials and apparatus, modeled on Montessori's didactic materials, that have critical feedback built in.

In a responsive environment, there is continuous critical interaction between each pupil's knowledge and the knowledge presented by the teacher, or in the matter of skills, between the pupils' skills and their consequences. With regard to theories, this critical interaction often takes the form of a critical dialogue where a pupil gives his criticisms of the theories presented, the teacher, or another pupil, gives counter-criticisms to the first pupil's criticisms, and so it goes, until all of the weaknesses, limitations, and errors have been explored. The function of a critical dialogue is not to justify one theory or another as true but rather to try to find out the mistakes, the errors, the inadequacies, the limitations in each and every theory set forth. Such critical dialogues at the very least probe and test pupils' present theories and at best help them to discover some of what is wrong with those theories.

So most classrooms should be devoted to critical dialogue, especially after pupils have reached the formal operational stage of cognitive development and are able to engage in logical arguments. But there are other ways teachers can create responsive environments. In science, for example, teachers can have pupils devise experiments to test a given theory or the criticisms made of a theory. In history, the teacher might suggest some research that would test and perhaps refute a theory or a criticism of a theory. In these cases, students spend much of the classroom time working out experiments and research programs and then discussing and criticizing the results.

Here I want to note that the Darwinian theory of education conceives all subject matters as having an objective existence. They are part of what Popper calls world three. There is, literally, a world of physics, a world of history, a world of mathematics, a world of swimming, a world of writing, a world of typing, and so on. Each of these domains consists of the problems and the tentative solutions—in the case of theories, it includes questions and arguments; in the case of skills, it includes moves and styles—that people have created in a particular field or area. All these different subject matters constitute part of what we call culture. Culture exists apart from people: it has an objective existence. Moreover, it can grow, evolve. And the way it evolves is through Darwinian selection.

At this point, we can begin to see the similarities between teaching and research. In both engagements, the procedure is one of uncovering and eliminating errors. In teaching, the teacher begins with the present (trial) knowledge of the student. In research, the researcher begins with the present (trial) knowledge current in the field—the state of the field. Both the teacher and the researcher then try to criticize that knowledge in the attempt to discover its inadequacies or errors. This criticism leads to the modification or refinement of the existing knowledge. In the case of teaching, it is the student who refines or modifies his own knowledge; in the case of research, it is the researcher himself, or other scholars in the field, who modify the existing knowledge in light of the unrefuted criticism.

If I am correct in this, and teaching and research are both selection procedures of trial-and-error elimination, then one of the advantages of the approach to teaching I have suggested here is that students from the beginning become participants in the research enterprise. From the beginning they understand that all knowledge is conjectural—created by fallible human beings. And they further understand that this means that knowledge can never be justified but can be improved—continually—through criticism. From the beginning of his educational career, then, each student is initiated as a participant in the advancement of knowledge.

When the subject matter consists of skills like painting, typing, swimming, or singing, the critical feedback comes from the model or the exemplar, or the demonstration that the teacher presents. The pupil recognizes that his trial efforts are not as successful as the model presented. By comparing what he does with the model, the pupil can discover his mistakes and try to eliminate them in subsequent trials.

In the case of skills, the teacher does not usually have to tell the pupil that his work is inadequate: the pupil knows that he reads poorly, types slowly, paints sloppily, or boxes ineffectively. What the pupil does not know is why the results of his trials are inadequate. He does not know what he is doing wrong. Here the teacher tries to locate the concrete actions that lead to the unwanted consequences. "By doing *this*, you are causing *that*. You don't want *that*, so something's wrong with doing *this*."

The teacher of skills does not tell the pupil what to do or how to do it. But he does help him to discover what he is doing wrong and then allows him to modify his efforts in light of that discovery. Becoming a better reader, speller, typist, swimmer, or carpenter is always a matter of modifying one's existing skills in light of their discovered inadequacies.

Critical feedback is the heart of the educational transaction. It must be if I am correct in assuming that pupils create knowledge by modifying their present knowledge when they discover its inadequacies. Without critical feedback, no learning can take place—there can be no growth in knowledge. I suggest, therefore, that whenever learning does take place in any classroom, it happens because of critical feedback. There is never any transmission of knowledge. This is an illusion—like an optical illusion. All learning is a modification of present knowledge.

Take the example of a pupil learning to spell a word, say, "cat." The teacher writes the word on the board, asks the pupil to copy it (imitate it), and then, later, asks him to reproduce it (from memory). When the pupil does so, it *looks* as if the teacher transmitted knowledge of how to spell the word "cat" to the pupil. What happened here, however, I suggest, is that the pupil modified his existing skills and understandings, thereby creating this new skill. Note: prior to the incident with the teacher, the pupil could speak and knew how to say and use the word "cat" appropriately; he knew the sounds and could identify and perhaps make the letters "a," "t," "c"; he knew how to hold a pencil and how to use it to make marks on paper. In possession of all these skills, the pupil could, when invited by the teacher, make a trial effort at writing the word "cat." This trial effort was a modification of his present skills and understandings. Moreover, the pupil probably made an inadequate showing on the first trial. The model on the chalkboard, or the model in his textbook, as the pupil interpreted it, would provide critical feedback to help him discover in what ways his attempt was inadequate. Additional practice (continuing trial-and-error elimination activity) results in improved performance.

In learning how to spell the word "cat," therefore, there was no transmission but simply a procedure of trial-and-error elimination conducted by the pupil. The teacher created a free environment that invited him to present his skills and understandings. The model presented by the teacher both educed the pupil's existing skills and also served as a source of critical feedback to him so that he could discover the inadequacies or msitakes in his own performance.

Thus, although transmission does not exist and all learning is the modification of existing knowledge in light of its discovered errors, this modification procedure *looks like* transmission, and as a result, many, perhaps most teachers think that they are in the transmission business. And although transmission never occurs, pupils *do* learn in "transmission" classrooms. But they learn not through transmission; they learn, as always, through the procedure of trial-and-error elimination.

In "transmission" classrooms, teachers do create environments that are somewhat free, responsive, and supportive. But they do not do this consciously and deliberately. It happens because of the logic of the situation. That is, no teacher, no matter how authoritarian or intimidating, can create an environment totally unfree. In every classroom, pupils can always to some degree disclose their present knowledge. Moreover, most teachers do create a supportive environment for students—often, however, only for the "good" students. Finally, would-be transmitter teachers do provide critical feedback to pupils. In classrooms run by would-be transmitter teachers, the pupil takes the subject matter as presented by the teacher as a tacit critical feedback to his own present knowledge, which knowledge he then covertly modifies accordingly. A would-be transmitter teacher supplies critical feedback in other ways: question and answer sessions, discussions, outside readings, homework, quizzes, tests, and examinations, which all help students to discover their mistakes.

But if transmission classrooms do work, if learning does occur, then why bother to revamp and reconstruct the role of the teacher? Why not let teachers continue to be would-be transmittters of knowledge? My answer is that although teachers who are would-be transmitters of knowledge do facilitate learning, they do not facilitate as much as they might.

Let me point out some serious drawbacks or limitations inherent in "transmission" classrooms. As I previously noted, they are coercive. Furthermore, the learning that they promote is both limited and largely accidental. Finally, "transmission" classrooms discriminate in favor of fast learners.

In classrooms run by wouuld-be transmitters, pupils receive the message loud and clear: in the matter of skills, these pupils hear the teacher saying, explicitly or implicitly: "Do it this way! Do it my way!" In the matter of understandings, they hear the teacher saying, explicitly or implicitly: "This is the correct understanding! Understand this the way I understand it!" Because they engage in what pupils perceive as coercive practices, would-be transmitter teachers produce a number of widely recognized and universally lamented pupil types.

First, there are those pupils who withdraw, either from fear or from resentment of the coercion. They do not participate in the trial-and-error elimination and so do not improve those skills and understandings of concern to the teachers. The teacher classifies them as the stupid ones.

Second, there are those pupils for whom schooling becomes a game—the game of finding out what the teacher *wants* and then fabricating those skills or understandings. These are the hipsters, those who create pseudo-knowledge, knowledge created especially for the teacher, which, in the course of events, usually disappears—after the test.

The third group are the true believers. These are the pupils who have undergone intellectual socialization. They regard the teacher (or the textbook, or the experts in the field) as final authorities, and they modify their own knowledge into accord with whatever pronouncements the authorities promulgate. (I suspect that many of these true believers find teaching [construed as transmission of true knowledge] an attractive occupation. Lord knows, they are in abundance among us.)

Having created these pupil types by construing their role as one of transmission, these same teachers often sincerely lament their presence in the classroom because, they complain, you "can't really teach" pupils who are stupid, or who are hipsters, or who are true believers.

The most salient drawback to the transmission classroom is that the focus is all wrong. The would-be transmitter teacher assumes that pupils are more or less passive receptors of knowledge, not active creators. Therefore, whatever critical feedback a pupil gets about his own knowledge is accidental, intermittent, haphazard, and usually judgmental. These factors all reduce and decrease the possibility that the transmitter teacher will facilitate the growth of the pupil's knowledge. (This gives some credence to the accusation that pupils [in transmission classrooms] learn in spite of their teachers.)

Another drawback to the transmission approach is that it curtails or limits the critical encounter between the pupil's present knowledge and the subject matter. In a transmission classroom, it is the pupil who determines the range, the depth, and the intensity of the critical encounter between his present knowledge and the subject matter content presented by the teacher. The pupil ascertains what conflicts there are between the subject matter and his present knowledge. Understandably—since errors are aversive to human beings—the pupil on his own will uncover only a limited number of conflicts. The upshot of this is that his self-limited critical encounter will restrict the changes or modifications he makes in his present knowledge. Moreover, such conflicts that he uncovers and the changes that he actually makes may be superficial. (This helps to explain why the minds of many pupils, including some who get "good marks," seem to be so unaffected by their schooling.)

In a nontransmission classroom, where pupils can make public their present knowledge and where critical feedback is a deliberately designed part of the educational transaction, it is the teacher who controls the rigor, depth, and intensity of the critical encounter between the subject matter content and the pupils' present knowledge. Having a better understanding of the subject matter, the teacher can more readily recognize mistakes in the pupils' present knowledge. In this kind of classroom, the teacher can design and use materials, problems, questions, and so forth that will help the pupil to recognize these mistakes.

Let me use a metaphor to explain this difference in the mode of critical feedback provided by transmission classrooms in comparison with the mode of critical feedback provided in a nontransmission classroom where the environment is free and responsive. In a transmission classroom, the pupil uses his own present knowledge as a searchlight to probe whatever the teacher presents, say, Newton's theory, or Shakespeare's *Hamlet*. In a classroom where the environment is free and responsive, the *teacher* uses Newton's theory or Shakespeare's *Hamlet* as a searchlight to probe the pupils' present knowledge. Since I view the educational transaction as an engagement to help the pupil improve his present knowledge, and since I see such improvement consisting of the discovery and elimination of mistakes in that present knowledge, then having the teacher use the subject matter as a searchlight to probe the pupils' present knowledge better facilitates the procedure of education.

A related and more obvious defect of the transmission classroom is the learning pace it imposes on pupils. In transmission classrooms, many pupils have very little time to discover and eliminate the mistakes in their present knowledge. The standard organization of class learning units and the usual practice of lecture, followed by questions, followed by assignments, followed by test, allows time for only the fastest learners to modify their learnings. Transmission classrooms, therefore, discriminate in favor of fast learners.

As I understand it, this is the exciting discovery made by Benjamin Bloom and his colleagues. What they have called mastery learning, I suggest, is an approach to teaching that has teachers create educative environments that are free and responsive, environments in which pupils can endlessly engage in trial-and-error elimination, trying out their present knowledge, discovering their mistakes, and eliminating those mistakes in the next trial. (I would also suggest that it is this possibility of endless trial-and-error elimination that explains the successful improvement of knowledge that takes place with programmed instruction and with the Montessori didactic materials.)

The notion of endless trial-and-error elimination brings me to my final aspect of an educative environment. For in addition to being free and (critically) responsive, an educative environment should be supportive.

As I understand it, a supportive environment is necessary for the growth of knowledge. For when students uncover mistakes in their present knowledge, they often get upset, dismayed, frightened, anxious. Instead of trying to modify or change their knowledge, they may become dogmatic, or they may even regress. A supportive environment can prevent this. It helps students to try again, to continually modify their knowledge in light of its discovered errors.

In a supportive environment, pupils readily recognize and accept their errors and mistakes; they readily admit that their theories are wrong, their skills inadequate. In a supportive environment, pupils do not fear making mistakes; instead, they look for mistakes. For this, they realize, is how they can improve their present knowledge. They are able to separate, or distance, their "selves" from their knowledge, able to view their knowledge as something objective, apart, something that can be changed, modified, improved.

With regard to the construction of a supportive environment, much depends upon the attitudes of the teacher. The teacher must be person-centered: concerned with helping the pupil improve his knowledge, not concerned with evaluating, judging, grading the pupil. To help the pupil, the teacher must be empathic, must try to understand matters as the pupil understands them. Teachers, of course, cannot always do this, but if the pupil sees that the teacher is trying, this itself helps to create a supportive environment.

Teachers should praise students, compliment them on their work. "Good," "fine," "excellent," "marvelous," "great" are words that teachers should use liberally and frequently. Marva Collins has worked wonders with her paeans of praise for her pupils. Teachers can and should always look for what is praiseworthy in pupils' work and let them know it. It is important to note, however, that this positive feedback is not directly educative; it does not promote growth since it does not lead to the modification of present knowledge. But positive feedback does indirectly promote growth by creating a supportive environment that makes the student more ready and able to receive and accept the critical feedback that *does* lead to the modification of his present knowledge.

In addition to the attitudes of the teacher, a supportive environment must be based upon a reconceptualization of the educational engagement, a reconceptualization along the Darwinian lines I have already sketched. Pupils are reassured and do feel supported when the teacher shares these conceptions with them.

First, take the Darwinian conception of the subject matter content, with its implication for the educational transaction. Pupils are relieved when the teacher admits that the subject matter is conjectural; that history is nothing more than the conjectures of fallible historians, physics the conjectures of fallible physicists, that typing, swimming, writing, indeed, all skills are simply human creations, experiments, that have been modified and changed over time because they were found lacking and that will continue to be modified and changed. And pupils become more at ease when they hear the teacher announce that they will not be expected to "learn," "master," "memorize," or "reproduce" the subject matter that will be presented but that instead they will be expected to encounter that subject matter critically, do do battle with it. They become less fearful of the subject matter when told that it is there simply as an agenda, something to educe or evoke their own knowledge, something to surpass.

This new conception of the content of education is intrinsically tied to the Darwinian conception of the nature of the pupil with its implications for the aims of education. And here pupils find it reassuring to be told that the aim of the course is the improvement of their present knowledge, since this implies that they do have some knowledge and indicates that the educational journey will begin at their present level of understanding while also holding out the optimistic notion that they can improve their present knowledge. They are even more reassured when told that there are no final goals, aims, or objectives for all to meet and be guided by, for improvement is endless and the sole concern of the course is that their knowledge continue to get better throughout the term or the year. "Getting better" means making fewer mistakes. And they are intrigued, although they might not fully understand it, when the teacher tells them that the improvement of knowledge takes place through the procedure of trial-and-error elimination. They appreciate the notion that we learn from our mistakes but always remain suspicious when told that schools and classrooms are places where people are supposed to make mistakes.

In addition to sharing with pupils the Darwinian conception of the nature of the pupil and the Darwinian conception of the content of education, the teacher can make the environment even more supportive by sharing with them the Darwinian conception of the role of the teacher. Pupils welcome the announcement that the teacher's role is not to judge, evaluate, classify, or grade them, but they are usually incredulous. And they are curious but mystified when told that the teacher's role is to create an educative environment, a classroom where they can learn from their mistakes.

All this mystifies them because this reconceptualization of the role of the teacher does seem to require actual participation in such an environment. Yet most pupils are willing to give this Darwinian construction of education a try. They like being treated as active creators of knowledge rather than passive receptors of knowledge. And they cotton more to teachers who give them freedom and who are responsive and supportive. And insofar as they do make public their present knowledge, are open to critical feedback, do engage critical dialogue, and do modify their knowledge in light of the unrefuted criticisms, they do grow.

It should be clear by now that I have no recipes for being a Darwinian teacher, no list of things to do on Monday to help pupils learn from their mistakes. Being a Darwinian teacher is primarily a matter of conceptual change, adopting conceptions of the teacher, the pupil, and the subject matter that are radically different from those normally held by most teachers. The actual methods, strategies, tactics, and moves that teachers can use to promote intellectual growth will best come from practicing teachers who have reconceived education as a procedure of growth instead of a process of transmission.

Promoting Moral-Social Growth

In the realm of moral-social growth, the teacher tries to create a free environment wherein pupils can act and interact in ways they are accustomed to. The teacher is not out to socialize them, or to impose "school" conduct on them, or to manage or control them, but rather to help them to improve *their* normal ways of interacting with others. To do this, the teacher must first create an environment where the pupil feels free to disclose his normal habitual, everyday conduct.

To do this, the teacher must try, as Neill said, to fit the classroom to the child. This means that the teacher must abandon all preconceptions about how pupils should behave and simply accept them as they are. Teachers should have positive regard for pupils as human beings. More than this, Rogers insists, teachers should prize pupils, each one as a unique individual. In such an open, accepting, caring climate, people will freely disclose their current modes of behavior.

But although the environment is free, this does not mean there are no rules. Every social organization has rules of conduct, and as Neill has shown, the basic rule or principle in a school is that no one may trespass on the freedom of others. From this basic principle, every classroom and school derives other, more concrete rules designed to protect the freedom of each and every member. This basic principle and the corollary rules derived from it guarantee that the school and classroom environment will be responsive. For when all subscribe to this basic principle, anyone who is adversely affected by the actions of another can criticize that person's conduct: all pupils receive critical feedback to their conduct when that conduct hurts others.

Although Neill insisted that all pupils should participate in making the rules that derive from the basic principle of not trespassing on the freedom of others, I don't think that such total participation is necessary. The staff can make the rules, or they can be made by committees made up of staff members and pupils. What is necessary is that all pupils be aware of the existence of such rules so that they can use them to protect themselves. Moreover, all schools should have some institutional arrangement, like Summerhill's General Meeting, where pupils can bring up transgressions of the rules and adjudicate them. Here, too, they could criticize the rules and have them modified in light of the criticisms. For in addition to knowing what the rules are, pupils must understand that fallible human beings have made the rules; so the rules are not perfect, they can be improved—via criticism.

The rules derived from the basic principle will vary from school to school and with the ages of the pupils. What is important to make clear is that the rules are primarily educative, not management rules. The rules are there to help pupils become self-regulating; they are not there to help the staff run an efficient institution. Pupils use the rules to protect themselves. But more than this, the employment of these rules by students to criticize the conduct of other students helps those other students to modify their conduct—helps them to become better. Moreover, living in such a self-regulating community increases the moral and social sensitivity of the members so that they all become self-regulating individuals.

But for this to happen the environment must also be supportive. In a supportive environment, a pupil is able to recognize and accept that he has made an error or mistake, admit that his conduct is inadequate—admit that it did adversely affect others. In a supportive environment, pupils are not defensive or evasive about their conduct. Nor are they indifferent, careless, or calloused. In a supportive environment, pupils become genuinely concerned not to hurt others and ready to change or modify their conduct when it does.

The creation of a supportive environment in part depends upon the attitudes of the teacher. As Rogers points out, the teacher must have empathic understanding, always trying to see the situation from the pupil's own point of view. The supportive teacher never condemns the pupil, never rejects him, dismisses him, or puts him down. He condemns the act (not the person), but only if and when the pupil can distance himself from his acts so that he can "take" criticism of the act and not "take it personally."

The teacher can also help to create a supportive environment by sharing with pupils his conception of human beings—and pupils. Human beings, he can explain, are fallible creatures who, no matter how hard they try, will act in ways that cause pain and hurt to others. But because they are fallible, they can always get better, they can modify their conduct when other people give them critical feedback. This is why we all need other people: as critics, so that with their help we can get better.

Promoting Psychological Growth

As we saw, Rogers identified three sources for psychological problems: when a person's behavior becomes inconsistent with his theory of self; when he perceives discrepancies within his theory of self; and when his self no longer functions adequately in the reality situation. All of us have at various times experienced these kinds of psychological problems—often they occurred in our youth, while we were in school. So we know that at least some of our pupils must experience them, too. The resolution of these problems is a matter of psychological growth: we create better, more adequate, more veracious theories of self. Teachers can facilitate such psychological growth by creating environments that are free, responsive, and supportive.

As we saw when discussing the theories of Carl Rogers, such an environment is largely the result of the teacher's attitudes, the result of the interpersonal relations the teacher sets up between the pupil and himself. At the outset, however, it must be clear that the teacher is not a therapist. The teacher is not qualified to treat pupils with emotional disorders or psychological problems. The teacher should refer such cases to qualified professional therapists. The teacher's role in the realm of psychological growth is simply to help pupils improve their understandings of themselves—just as teachers help pupils improve their understandings of the physical universe and the social world they inhabit.

In many and various ways, pupils daily reveal their theories of self: in what they say, how they say it, when they say it; in what they write; in how they stand, sit, walk. In the face of such revelations, the teacher should be accepting, no matter how strange, wierd, unseemly, inaccurate, or toe curling they might be. The pupil's theory of self will probably be inadequate, incomplete, false. But the teacher must create a climate, a freedom, that allows the pupil to disclose it. If possible, the teacher should prize the real person beyond the theory of self that the pupil presents publicly. He must disclose his own trust that the pupil can modify his present theories about himself, can improve them.

   The teacher can facilitate this by being responsive to the pupil's presentation of his theory of self. Here the response consists primarily of feeding back to the pupil the objective content of what he reveals—in speech, writing, and body language: "You seem to feel . . . today." This should not be done in a censurious manner but simply as an expression of concern, of caring about how the pupil does feel.

   But in addition to feeding back to the pupil the theories of self he discloses, the teacher responds with expressions of his own feelings. The teacher must be congruent, to use Rogers's term: the teacher must be aware of his feelings and able to express those feelings to the pupil: "I like this." "This I find distasteful." By reflecting back the pupils' revealed theories of self and by revealing their own real feelings to pupils, teachers create a responsive environment that helps pupils discover the inadequacies in their present theories of self ("Am I really that kind of person?"). This discovery will lead to a modification of those theories and thus to better self-understanding.

   Being responsive can be painful, both for pupils and for teachers. This is mitigated when the environment is also supportive, when the teacher has empathic understanding for the pupil ("This is how I feel, but I can understand why you said what you did").

   Although it is part of the teacher's responsibility, promoting psychological growth is not, I think, the top priority in education, not even in elementary and secondary schools. And I fear that too much concern with it will displace and curtail the promotion of intellectual growth, which *is* the top priority of educational institutions.

FURTHER IMPLICATIONS OF THE DARWINIAN THEORY OF EDUCATION

   In this book I have dealt with the growth of knowledge, conduct, and self-understanding. But the Darwinian conception of growth applies to all that human beings create: to all of culture, all of world three. Human beings create social arrangements, economic arrangements, and political arrangements. So these, too, can grow. And they grow through the same Darwinian selection procedure of trial-and-error elimination. Fallible human beings have created our political, social, and economic arrangements, so they cannot be perfect, but they can be improved: via criticism. Through criticism, we can uncover their inadequacies and limitations.

This means that we can also use the growth metaphor to construct the social, political, and economic functions of schools. Traditionally, in line with the transmission conception of education, teachers have construed these functions as a process of socialization. Teachers set out to socialize students to *fit into* the existing arrangements: they prepare them to be citizens, workers, members of the society by imposing on them certain predetermined ideas, skills, understandings, beliefs, attitudes. The function of the school is taken to be the reproduction of the society by turning out people who will accept and maintain the existing social, political, and economic arrangements. This is authoritarian. It prevents improvement. Sometimes reformers have tried to use the schools to improve society. But caught in the spell of the transmission theory, they could only come up with another version of socialization: in this case, socialization to some ideal society, some ideal polity, some ideal economic system. Schooling remained authoritarian.

If, however, we view the existing social, political, and economic arrangements as part of world three, as imperfect creations of fallible human beings that can always be improved via criticism, then we can construe new functions for the school. Instead of socializing students, we can try to educate them to become concerned critics: critical citizens, critical workers, critical employers, critical consumers. So educated, students will emerge from school concerned with preserving and improving our existing arrangements and prepared to engage in the critical dialogue through which improvement takes place.

This brings us, finally, to the new conception of the aim of education provided by the Darwinian theory of education. As we saw, the aim of education of the earliest metaphor of education was to initiate the young into culture. With the latest metaphor, the aim is to facilitate the growth of culture, or what Popper calls world three. To do this, schools should attempt to develop in the young a responsibility for the culture, a responsibility for its nurture and growth. Since culture grows through criticism, the aim of education will be to prepare people to become concerned critics of the culture. To do this, the school can try to present as many different aspects of the culture to students as possible, present them as the creations of human beings, creations that are rational because they have withstood past criticisms, but creations that can continue to improve and grow through criticism.

. . .

A few last words on the practicability of the Darwinian theory of education. It is not a romantic theory of education. It does not assume that the student is naturally good or naturally wise. Instead, it assumes that students—all human beings—are fallible: we all make mistakes. But it insists that that is how we learn—from our mistakes: by eliminating or reducing our mistakes, our knowledge grows, as does our conduct, our self-concept, and our culture.

Nor does this Darwinian theory of education require a reconstruction of the existing educational arrangements in our schools before it can be implemented. What it calls for is a reconceptualization of education in terms of the metaphor of growth, construing growth as a procedure of trial-and-error elimination. This construction of education entails, as I have shown, a reconceptualization of the content of education, the role of the student, the role of the teacher, and the aim of education. But I believe that all these conceptual changes can begin to take place within the existing arrangements of most schools. It is true that the present arrangements in most schools were all erected under the influence of the transmission metaphor of education. However, within these existing arrangements teachers can promote intellectual growth, for the following reasons:

1. It is possible to *present* the subject matter rather than try to transmit it.
2. It is possible to invite students to *encounter* the subject matter critically rather than to try to get them to accept it.
3. It is possible to view these critical encounters as a selection procedure of *trial-and-error elimination* wherein knowledge grows.
4. Regardless of institutional constraints, teachers can facilitate this growth by construing their role to be that of creating a classroom environment that is more free, more responsive, and more supportive: a place where students can more readily learn from their mistakes.
5. Finally, it is possible, in the schools as they presently are, for teachers to reconceptualize the aim of schooling as an attempt to develop concerned critics who can and will facilitate the growth of our culture.

NOTES

CHAPTER 1: THREE METAPHORS FOR EDUCATION

1. John Amos Comenius, *The Great Didactic* (London: Adam and Charles Black, 1896), p. 441.
2. Thomas Elyot, *The Boke Named the Governor* (1531) (London: J. M. Dent and Sons, 1962), p. 13.
3. Francis Bacon, *The Advancement of Learning* (1605) (London: J. M. Dent and Sons, 1958), p. 34.
4. John Amos Comenius, *The Orbis Pictus* (1672) (Syracuse, N.Y.: C. W. Bardeen 1887), p. xiv, author's preface.
5. Jean Jacques Rousseau, *Emile* (1760) (London: J. M. Dent and Sons, 1957), p. 5.

CHAPTER 2: KARL POPPER'S EVOLUTIONARY EPISTEMOLOGY

1. See Eric Havelock, *The Greek Concept of Justice* (Cambridge, Mass.: Harvard University Press, 1978), chapter 18.
2. See K. R. Popper, *Conjectures and Refutations* (London: Routledge & Kegan Paul, 1963); Paul A. Schlipp, ed., *The Philosophy of Karl Popper* (LaSalle,

Ill.: Open Court, 1974), especially part 1, "Autobiography"; and K. R. Popper, *Objective Knowledge* (Oxford: Oxford University Press, 1972).

3. Karl Popper, "Autobiography," in Schlipp, *The Philosophy of Karl Popper*, p. 28.

4. Popper, *Objective Knowledge*, p. 109.

5. Karl R. Popper and John C. Eccles, *The Self and Its Brain* (New York: Springer International, 1977), p. 40.

6. See Ernest Gombrich, *A Sense of Order* (Ithaca, N.Y.: Cornell University Press, 1979), chapter 1.

7. Popper, *Conjectures and Refutations*, p. 44.

8. Popper, *Objective Knowledge*, p. 346.

9. Ibid., p. 346.

10. Ibid., pp. 119–20 and p. 120 n.8.

11. Ibid., p. 25.

12. Schlipp, *The Philosophy of Karl Popper*, p. 1020.

13. Popper, *Objective Knowledge*, p. 24.

14. Popper, *Conjectures and Refutations*, p. 45.

15. Schlipp, *The Philosophy of Karl Popper*, p. 1015.

16. Ibid., p. 1020.

17. Ibid., p. 142.

18. K. R. Popper, "The Rationality of Scientific Revolutions," in Rom Harre, ed., *Problems of Scientific Revolutions* (Oxford: Clarendon Press, 1975), p. 96 n.21. Also see Popper, *Objective Knowledge*, p. 261.

19. Popper, *Objective Knowledge*, p. 246.

20. Ibid., p. 119.

CHAPTER 3: JEAN PIAGET

1. Psychologists all over the world have replicated Piaget's experiments. For the most part, these attempts have corroborated his original analysis of the periods of cognitive development. Much of the criticisms other psychologists have made of Piaget's work revolve around questions of competence versus performance. The critics argue that the so-called different periods of cognitive development merely indicate the presence or absence of specific performance skills, which are learned. They reject Piaget's contention that different stages of development indicate the presence or absence of specific competencies that "emerge" at specific points of cognitive development. Those who favor a performance theory have conducted numerous experiments that show that specific kinds of behaviors can and do appear in some children earlier than Piaget says they do. This, they argue, indicates that these behaviors are learned. (Many of these replication experiments are summarized in Charles J. Brainerd, *Piaget's Theory of Intelligence* (Englewood Cliffs, N.J.: Prentice-Hall, 1978); see

also Irving E. Siegel and Frank H. Hooper, eds., *Logical Thinking in Children* (New York: Holt, Rinehart and Winston, 1968). Other criticisms of Piaget's theory are in L. S. Siegel and C. J. Brainerd, eds., *Alternatives to Piaget: Critical Essays on the Theory* (New York: Academic Press, 1978).

I do not think that these criticisms seriously impair the validity of Piaget's work. No critic has disproved the existence of the four periods of cognitive development. It is true that there are variations in the rate of speed at which children from different cultures, children with different experiences, and children of different intelligence go through the four periods of development. However, the sequence of stages is invariant: the second stage always follows the first, the third the second, the fourth the third, and no stage can be skipped. Moreover, later stages incorporate, or are based on, earlier stages. Finally, I think that the primary worth of Piaget's theory does not lie with the so-called cognitive stages of development but rather, as I shall show in the text, in his conception of human beings as creators of their knowledge.

2. Piaget's main works on these periods of development include *The Origins of Intelligence in Children* (New York: Norton, 1963); *Play, Dreams and Imitation in Childhood* (New York: Norton, 1962); *The Early Growth of Logic in the Child* (New York: Norton, 1969); and *The Growth of Logical Thinking from Childhood to Adolescence*, with Barbel Inhelder (London: Routledge & Kegan Paul, 1958).

3. "The two main functions of the intelligence are to invent and to understand." (Piaget, *Biology and Knowledge* [Chicago: University of Chicago Press, 1971], p. 213.) Piaget himself does not use the term "theory," but instead refers to "schemes" and "concepts." A concept, he explains, "is nothing but a scheme of action and operation." (*La Psychologie de l'intelligence* [Paris: Cohn, 1947], p. 41). He distinguishes between the "schemes" our sensory-motor acts create (schemes like grasping and pulling) and the "concepts" our logical operations create (concepts like conversation). I prefer to call both schemes and concepts "theories." (It may be helpful to regard sensory-motor theories [schemes like grasping and pulling] as "how-to" theories.)

4. In most discussions of this experiment, commentators argue that pre-operational children do not possess the concept of conservation. But Piaget has shown that preoperational children, and even sensory-motor children, do conserve. "Object permanence" is a form of conservation (recall his daughter and the vanished pocket watch). Moreover, Piaget has actually said that conservation is based on identity (*The Child's Conception of Geometry* with Barbel Inhelder and Alina Szeminska [New York: Basic Books, 1960], p. 102). Piaget suggests that "conservation" is based on reversibility. If the child cannot perform reverse cognitive operations, then she cannot conserve. Thus, a watch no longer visible cannot become visible again; hence, it cannot exist. The child cannot conserve. Objects have no permanence. Again, the water in this tall, thin glass is more than it was when it was in the short, fat glass. The

child cannot conserve quantity. Operational thought, Piaget says, consists of operations that are reversible, for example, addition and subtraction, or the inverse relationship between the diameter of a glass and the height of the water. In my interpretation of the water-in-the-glass experiment, I am suggesting that preoperational children can conserve because they do have a theory of identity—a perceptual theory of identity. But this perceptual theory of identity enables them to conserve only properties that do not change in appearance, for example, the color or the shape of a block of wood. (This is what Piaget means by "object permanence." These children cannot conserve properties that do change in appearance—such as the quantity of water in glasses of different diameter—because these are relational changes and preoperational children cannot create relational theories through which they could understand such changes. They cannot create relational theories because such theories are always reversible [if A = B, then B = A], and preoperational children cannot perform these operations.)

5. Piaget, *Play, Dreams and Imitation in Childhood*, p. 224.

6. See Jean Piaget, *The Child's Conception of the World* (London: Routledge & Kegan Paul, 1929); *The Child's Conception of Physical Causality* (London: Routledge & Kegan Paul, 1930); *The Construction of Reality in the Child* (New York: Basic Books, 1970); with Barbel Inhelder, *The Origin of the Idea of Change in Children* (New York: Norton, 1975); The Child's Conception of Number (New York: Norton, 1975).

7. Piaget, *The Construction of Reality in the Child*, pp. 231–32.

8. Ibid., p. 261.

9. Ibid., p. 258.

10. Piaget, *The Child's Conception of the World*, p. 220.

11. Jean Piaget, *Judgment and Reasoning in the Child* (New York: Harcourt Brace, 1928), p. 229.

12. Jean Piaget, *The Child's Conception of Physical Causality*, p. 228.

13. Ibid., p. 229.

14. Ibid., pp. 62, 65, 71, 72.

15. John Flavell, who has written the most comprehensive exposition of Piaget's developmental psychology, has likened Piaget's notion of cognitive assimilation to the notion of the late American psychologist George Kelly, who claimed that human beings *construe* reality, which means that they create a mental construct of the situations they encounter. John M. Flavell, *The Developmental Psychology of Jean Piaget* (New York: Van Nostrand, 1963), p. 48.

16. See Jean Piaget, *Behavior and Evolution* (New York: Pantheon Books, 1978), pp. xvi, 6, 22–23.

17. See Jean Piaget, *Structuralism* (New York: Basic Books, 1971), chapter 4, especially p. 63; also, Piaget, *The Origins of Intelligence in Children*, pp. 185–86.

18. Piaget, *Biology and Knowledge*, p. 12.

19. Piaget, *Behavior and Evolution*, pp. xvi, 6, 22–23; also Piaget, *Biology and Knowledge*, pp. 300–304.

20. Piaget, *The Construction of Reality in the Child*, p. 113.

21. Piaget, *The Origins of Intelligence in Children*, p. 26.

22. Ibid., pp. 27–28.

23. Piaget, *Play, Dreams and Imitation in Childhood*, p. 217.

24. Ibid., p. 216.

25. Ibid., p. 225.

26. Piaget, *The Child's Conception of Number*, p. 164.

27. Ibid., p. 176.

28. Jean Piaget, *Genetic Epistemology* (New York: Norton, 1970), pp. 27–28.

29. Jean Piaget, in *Play and Development*, ed. Maria W. Piers (New York: Norton, 1972), p. 27.

CHAPTER 4: B. F. SKINNER

1. Skinner distinguishes radical behaviorism from methodological behaviorism. Methodological behaviorism rejects feelings and states of mind as having anything to do with behavior. It does not deny that feelings and mental states exist, but because there could be no public agreement about their validity (How do you feel? What is he thinking?), methodological behaviorists ignore mental states and feelings in trying to explain behavior. Radical behaviorists do not rule out feelings and mental states, but they classify both as behavior, behavior that occurs inside the body. Feelings and mental states are not the cause of behavior according to radical behaviorists; rather, they are the internal products of a person's genetic and environmental histories.

2. B. F. Skinner, *The Technology of Teaching* (New York: Appleton-Century-Crofts, 1968), p. 14.

3. There is a vast literature on this. See, to begin with, F. M. Kanter and J. S. Philipps, *Learning Foundations of Behavior Therapy* (New York: Wiley, 1970); and T. M. Stephens, *Implementing Behavioral Approaches in Elementary and Secondary Schools* (Columbus, Ohio: Merrill, 1975); and N. K. Buckley and H. M. Walker, *Modifying Classroom Behavior* (Champagne, Ill.: Research Press, 1973).

4. B. F. Skinner, *About Behaviorism* (New York: Vintage Books, 1976).

5. Ibid., p. 41.

6. Ibid., p. 44.

7. Skinner, *The Technology of Teaching*, p. 66.

8. Ibid., p. 67.

9. Skinner, *About Behaviorism*, p. 123.

10. Ibid.

11. B. F. Skinner, *Beyond Freedom and Dignity* (New York: Bantam Books, 1972).

12. Ibid., pp. 121, 123.

13. Skinner, *About Behaviorism*, p. 221.

14. Ibid., p. 208.

15. In *About Behaviorism*, Skinner himself raises this objection to behaviorism, but his reply fails to rebut the criticism. See argument no. 15, pp. 5, 158–261.

16. Ibid., p. 82. Here is Skinner's more technical discussion of this: "Any stimulus present when an operant is reinforced acquires control in the sense that the rate will be higher when it is present. Such a stimulus does not act as a goad; it does not elicit the response in the sense of forcing it to occur. It is simply an essential aspect of the occasion upon which response is made and reinforced." (*Contingencies of Reinforcement: A Theoretical Analysis* [New York: Appleton-Century-Crofts, 1969], p. 7.)

17. Skinner, *About Behaviorism*, p. 53.

18. Ibid., p. 226.

19. Skinner, *The Technology of Teaching*, p. 45.

CHAPTER 5: MARIA MONTESSORI

1. Maria Montessori, *The Montessori Method* (New York: Schocken Books, 1964), p. 115.

2. John J. McDermott makes this point in his introduction to E. M. Standing's filiopietistic study, *Maria Montessori: Her Life and Work* (Fresno, Calif.: Academy Library Guild, 1959).

3. But see C. H. Patterson, *Foundations for a Theory of Instruction and Educational Psychology* (New York: Harper & Row, 1977), p. 62, who claims "although her practice developed from observation and experience rather than being derived from theory, the Montessori approach has a theoretical base." See also p. 56.

4. Maria Montessori, *The Absorbent Mind* (New York: Holt, Rinehart and Winston, 1967), pp. 246–47.

5. Montessori, *The Montessori Method*, p. 109.

6. Montessori, *Dr. Montessori's Own Handbook* (New York: F. A. Stokes, 1914), p. 27.

7. Ibid., p. 31.

8. Ibid., p. 77.

9. Montessori, *The Montessori Method*, p. 84.

10. Ibid., p. 85.

11. Montessori, *Dr. Montessori's Own Handbook*, p. 32.

12. Montessori, *The Absorbent Mind*, p. 246.

13. Montessori, *Dr. Montessori's Own Handbook*, p. 32.

14. Ibid.

15. Dewey, who thought that all problems posed in schools should be real problems, failed to appreciate the significance of Montessori's didactic materials. See John and Evelyn Dewey, *Schools of Tomorrow* (New York: Dutton, 1915), pp. 154–57.

16. Montessori, *The Absorbent Mind*, p. 249.

17. Ibid., p. 67.

18. Montessori, *The Montessori Method*, p. 228.

19. Ibid.

20. Neil Postman and Charles Weingartner, *Teaching as a Subversive Activity* (New York: Delacorte Press, 1969), passim.

21. See above. The section on conjectural knowledge in chapter 2 for discussion of the four functions of language.

22. Montessori, *The Montessori Method*, p. 109.

23. Ibid., p. 285.

24. Ibid., p. 287.

25. Ibid., p. 298.

26. Ibid., p. 304.

27. Montessori, *The Absorbent Mind*, p. 169.

28. Ibid., p. 282.

29. Montessori, *The Montessori Method*, pp. 105–6.

30. Maria Montessori, *Education and Peace* (Chicago: Regnery, 1972), p. 92.

31. Montessori, *The Montessori Method*, pp. 61–62 (italics in original).

32. Ibid., p. 71.

33. Montessori, *Dr. Montessori's Own Handbook*, p. 116.

34. Ibid., p. 26.

35. Montessori, *The Montessori Method*, pp. 348–49.

36. Ibid., p. 87.

37. Ibid., p. 88.

38. Ibid., pp. 92–93.

39. Ibid., p. 94.

40. Ibid., p. 337.

41. Montessori, *The Absorbent Mind*, p. 261.

42. Montessori, *The Montessori Method*, p. 349.

43. The Popper-Darwinian interpretation of Montessori's work that I have presented, while not Aristotelian, does rest upon the acceptance of realism. By this I mean that it assumes the existence of a real universe with an order inherent in it, although we fallible human beings can never (*pace* Aristotle and Montessori) know what the order is.

44. Montessori, *The Montessori Method*, p. 364.

CHAPTER 6: A. S. NEILL

1. *A Dominie in Doubt*, in *The Dominie Books of A. S. Neill* (New York: Hart, 1975), p. 146.

2. Ibid.

3. Quoted in Ray Hemmings, *Fifty Years of Freedom* (London: Allen & Unwin, 1972), p. 47.

4. A. S. Neill, *Summerhill: A Radical Approach to Child Rearing* (New York: Hart, 1960), p. 4.

5. Ibid.

6. When asked to explain the difference between Summerhill and a Montessori school, Neill explained: "A kid can say fuck in Summerhill, but not in a Montessori school." A. S. Neill, *Neill! Neill! Orange Peel!* (New York: Hart, 1972), p. 339.

7. Neill, *Summerhill*, p. 114.

8. Ibid., pp. 35–36.

9. A. S. Neill, *The Problem Child* (London: Jenkins, 1934), p. 217.

10. Neill, *Summerhill*, p. 48.

11. Ibid., p. 348.

12. Ibid., p. 107.

13. Ibid., p. 155.

14. Ibid., p. 167.

15. Ibid.

16. Ibid., p. 51.

17. Ibid., p. 250.

18. See Richard Sennett, *The Fall of Public Man* (New York: Vintage Books, 1978), pp. 216–323.

19. Quoted in Hemmings, *Fifty Years of Freedom*, p. 141.

20. Neill, *Neill! Neill! Orange Peel!* p. 247.

21. Ibid., p. 243.

22. Emanuel Bernstein, "Summerhill Graduates," *Psychology Today* (October 1968), pp. 37–40, 70.

23. Neill, *Summerhill*, p. 294. See also, Neill, *Neill! Neill! Orange Peel!* p. 225.

24. Ibid., p. 54.

25. Ibid., p. 297.

26. Ibid., p. 118.

27. Ibid., p. 284.

28. Ibid., p. 149.

29. Ibid., p. 4.

30. Ibid., p. 195.

31. Ibid., p. 119.

32. Ibid., p. 292.

CHAPTER 7: CARL ROGERS

1. See my *The Possibilities of Error* (New York: McKay, 1971).
2. Carl Rogers, *Client-Centered Therapy* (Boston: Houghton Mifflin, 1951), p. 24.
3. Ibid., p. 196.
4. Ibid., p. 192.
5. Ibid., p. 40.
6. Quoted in Howard Kirschenbaum, *On Becoming Carl Rogers* (New York: Delacorte Press, 1971), p. 121.
7. Ibid., p. 163.
8. Ibid., p. 196.
9. Quoted in Kirschenbaum, *On Becoming Carl Rogers*, pp. 166–67.
10. Rogers, *Client-Centered Therapy*, p. 389.
11. Carl Rogers, *Freedom to Learn* (Columbus, Ohio: Merrill, 1969), pp. 152–53.
12. Ibid., p. 110.
13. Carl Rogers, *Freedom to Learn*, 2nd ed. (Columbus, Ohio: Merrill, 1983), pp. 195–224.
14. Rogers, *Freedom to Learn* (1969), p. 46.
15. Ibid., pp. 103–4.
16. Ibid., p. 104.
17. Ibid., p. 153.
18. Ibid., pp. 250, 286–87.
19. Ibid., p. 251.
20. Ibid., pp. 157–58.
21. Ibid., pp. 159–62.

SELECTED BIBLIOGRAPHY

KARL R. POPPER

Popper's most famous and influential book in the philosophy of science is *Logik der Forschung* (Vienna: Springer, 1935), translated as *The Logic of Scientific Discovery* (London: Hutchinson, 1959). Recently he published *Postscript to the Logic of Scientific Discovery* in three volumes, edited by W. W. Bartley, III (London: Hutchinson, 1982). *Conjectures and Refutations* (London: Routledge & Kegan Paul, 1963/1968) contains a collection of his essays on the philosophy of science.

Popper is equally famous for his work on the philosophy of history and political theory. This includes *The Poverty of Historicism* (London: Routledge & Kegan Paul, 1944–45/1957), and *The Open Society and Its Enemies* (London: Routledge & Kegan Paul, 1945/1966).

Many of his essays on Darwinian epistemology appear in *Objective Knowledge* (Oxford: Oxford University Press, 1972/1979). He also coauthored, with J. C. Eccles, *The Self and Its Brain* (New York: Springer International, 1977).

A good introduction to Popper's philosophy is Brian Magee, *Popper* (London: Fontana/Collins, 1973). P. A. Schlipp edited *The Philosophy of Karl Popper* (LaSalle, Ill.: Open Court, 1974), a two-volume collection of criticisms and commentary on Popper's philosophy, together with Popper's replies. Two critical assessments of Popper's philosophy are R. Ackermann, *The Philosophy of Karl Popper* (Amherst: University of Massachusetts Press, 1976), and A. O'Hear, *Karl Popper* (London: Routledge & Kegan Paul, 1980).

Popper's intellectual autobiography is *Unended Quest* (London: Fontana, 1976).

JEAN PIAGET

Piaget authored and coauthored more than twenty books on child development. The three earliest, and most famous, were based on a day-by-day (hour-by-hour) observation of his own three children. They are *The Origins of Intelligence in Children* (New York: Norton, 1963); *The Construction of Reality in the Child* (New York: Basic Books, 1954); and *Play, Dreams and Imitation in Childhood* (New York: Norton, 1962).

Piaget also wrote books on the child's conception of time, space, movement, speed, number, physical causality, the world, and geometry, and he wrote *The Moral Judgment of the Child* (London: Kegan, Paul, 1932), *Judgment and Reasoning in the Child* (New York: Harcourt Brace, 1928), and *The Early Growth of Logic in the Child* (New York: Norton, 1969).

Two books by Piaget that present his overall theory and approach are *Genetic Epistemology* (New York: Norton, 1970), and *Six Psychological Studies* (New York: Vintage Books, 1968).

A good introduction to Piaget's thought is Howard Gardner, *The Quest for the Mind* (New York: Knopf, 1973). Other introductory books include Nathan Isaacs, *A Brief Introduction to Piaget* (New York: Schocken Books, 1972), P. G. Richmond, *An Introduction to Piaget* (New York: Basic Books, 1971), and the very lucid, Mary Ann Spencer Pulacki, *Understanding Piaget* (New York: Harper & Row, 1971). The most thorough coverage is still John H. Flavell, *The Developmental Psychology of Jean Piaget* (New York: Van Nostrand Reinhold, 1963). Also see Howard E. Gruber and J. Jacques Vonèche, *The Essential Piaget* (New York: Basic Books, 1977). In a class by itself is the delightful *Conversations with Piaget* by Jean Claude Bringuier (Chicago: University of Chicago Press, 1980).

Some books that provide critical assessments of Piaget's work are *New Directions in Piagetian Theory and Practice*, edited by I. E. Siegel et al. (Hillsdale, N.J.: L. Erlbaum, 1981), *Alternatives to Piaget: Critical Essays on the Theory*, edited by Linda S. Siegal and Charles J. Brainerd (New York: Academic Press, 1978), and Brian Rotman, *Jean Piaget: Psychologist of the Real* (Ithaca, N.Y.: Cornell University Press, 1978).

Piaget claimed not to be an educator, but he did publish two books on education: *To Understand Is to Invent* (New York: Viking Press, 1974), and *Science of Education and the Psychology of the Child* (New York: Viking Press, 1969).

A number of books try to show how Piaget can be applied in the classroom: Rodger W. Bybee, *Piaget for Educators* (Columbus, Ohio: Merrill, 1982); H. G. Furth, *Piaget for Teachers* (Englewood Cliffs, N.J.: Prentice-Hall, 1970);

H. G. Furth and H. Wachs, *Thinking Goes to School: Piaget's Theory in Practice* (New York: Oxford University Press, 1974); M. Schwebel and J. Raph, eds., *Piaget in the Classroom* (New York: Basic Books, 1973); F. B. Murray, ed., *The Impact of Piagetian Theory on Education, Psychiatry and Psychology* (Baltimore: University Park Press, 1979); and B. J. Wadsworth, *Piaget for the Classroom Teacher* (New York: McKay, 1977).

B. F. SKINNER

B. F. Skinner is undoubtedly the most influential figure in American psychology—and the most controversial. His most famous works are *The Behavior of Organisms* (New York: Appleton-Century-Crofts, 1938), and *Science and Human Behavior* (New York: Macmillan, 1953). He has written a fictional account of a utopian society based on the scientific control of human behavior, *Walden Two* (New York: Macmillan, 1948). His most controversial work is *Beyond Freedom and Dignity* (New York: Bantam Books, 1972), where he explains how we can, and why we must, employ behavior modification to cure the ills of our existing society. In *About Behaviorism* (New York: Vintage, 1976), he responds to his critics. His more technical works include *Verbal Behavior* (New York: Appleton-Century-Crofts, 1957), *Contingencies of Reinforcement* (New York: Appleton-Century-Crofts, 1969), and *Cumulative Record* (New York: Appleton-Century-Crofts, 1972), a collection of his published papers. He has applied his ideas to education in *The Technology of Teaching* (New York: Appleton-Century-Crofts, 1968). Skinner has published two volumes of his autobiography, *Particulars of My Life* (New York: McGraw-Hill, 1977), and *The Shaping of a Behaviorist* (New York: Knopf, 1979).

Some books about Skinner are Richard I. Evans, *B. F. Skinner: The Man and His Ideas* (New York: Holt, Rinehart and Winston, 1981), and Finley Carpenter, *The Skinner Primer* (Glencoe, Ill.: Free Press, 1974). Some books of interest to educators include K. D. O'Leary and S. G. O'leary, *Classroom Management* (New York: Pergamon Press, 1977); J. A. Poteet, *Behavior Modification: A Practical Guide for Teachers* (Minneapolis: Burgess, 1973); T. M. Stephens, *Implementing Behavioral Approaches in Elementary and Secondary Schools* (Columbus, Ohio: Merrill, 1975); NSSE 72nd Yearbook, *Behavioral Modification in Education* (Chicago: National Society for the Study of Education, 1972); Walter Kolesnick, *Humanism and/or Behaviorism in Education* (Boston: Allyn and Bacon, 1974).

The most acute and persistent critic of Skinner's behaviorism has been Noam Chomsky. See his "The Case Against B. F. Skinner," in *For Reasons of State* (New York: Pantheon Books, 1971). Also see Michael Scriven, "The Philosophy of Behaviorism," in NSSE 72nd Yearbook, *Behavioral Modification in Education* (Chicago: National Society for the Study of Education, 1972).

MARIA MONTESSORI

Fourteen of Maria Montessori's books have been translated into English. The most important are *The Montessori Method* (New York: Schocken Books, 1964), *Dr. Montessori's Own Handbook* (New York: Schocken Books, 1965), *The Absorbent Mind* (New York: Holt, Rinehart and Winston, 1967), and *Spontaneous Activity in Education* (New York: Schocken Books, 1965).

Many books have been written about her method. Two of the more comprehensive are E. M. Standing, *Maria Montessori: Her Life and Work* (Fresno, Calif.: Academy Guild Press, 1959), and P. O. Lillard, *Montessori: A Modern Approach* (New York: Schocken Books, 1972).

A historically relevant critique of Montessori is in John and Evelyn Dewey's *Schools of Tomorrow* (New York: Dutton, 1915), chapter 6. In addition, there are W. H. Kilpatrick, *The Montessori System Examined* (Boston: Houghton Mifflin, 1914), and Nancy Rambusch, *Learn How to Learn* (Baltimore: Helicon Press, 1962).

There are national and international Montessori periodicals, Montessori societies, training colleges, and firms that sell Montessori materials, as well as Montessori films. E. M. Standing's book lists many of these in an appendix.

Rita Kramer has written a perceptive biography, *Maria Montessori* (New York: Putnams, 1976).

A. S. NEILL

A. S. Neill wrote twenty-one books. The first, *A Dominie's Log*, appeared in 1915. Three of his Dominie books were published by his American publisher, *The Dominie Books of A. S. Neill* (New York: Hart, 1975). His most famous books are *Summerhill: A Radical Approach to Education* (New York: Hart, 1960); *The Free Child* (London: Herbert Jenkins, 1949); and *Freedom—Not License!* (New York: Hart, 1966).

J. Walmsey has written about the school in *Neill and Summerhill* (Baltimore: Penguin, 1969). Also see H. Smitzer, *Living at Summerhill* (New York: Collier Books, 1968), and Joshua Popenoe, *Inside Summerhill* (New York: Hart, 1970). R. Skidelsky has a good analysis of the man and his ideas in *English Progressive Schools* (Baltimore: Penguin, 1969). For a history and analysis of Summerhill, see R. Hemmings, *Children's Freedom* (New York: Schocken Books, 1973).

H. Hart has edited *Summerhill: For and Against* (New York: Hart, 1970), a collection of commentaries and criticisms of Summerhill.

Neill's autobiography is *Neill! Neill! Orange Peel!* (New York: Hart, 1972).

A full-length biography by Jonathan Choall, *Neill of Summerhill* (New York: Pantheon, 1983) appeared after this manuscript had gone to press, as did the companion volume by Jonathan Choall, *All the Best, Neill: Letters from Summerhill* (New York: Franklin Watts, 1984).

CARL ROGERS

Carl Rogers is one of the founders of what is called humanistic psychology. The other leading figures are Rollo May and the late Abraham Maslow. This movement has its roots in the philosophical position called phenomenology. Whereas the behaviorist orientation considers man to be a passive organism governed by stimuli supplied by the external environment, the phenomenological orientation considers man to be the source of all acts: man is free to make choices in each situation.

These two approaches are explored in *Behaviorism and Phenomenology: Contrasting Bases for Modern Psychology*, edited by T. W. Mann (Chicago: University of Chicago Press, 1964). Also see Frank Milhollan and Bill E. Forisha, *From Skinner to Rogers: Contrasting Approaches to Education* (Lincoln, Neb.: Professional Educators, 1972).

Carl Rogers's book on person-centered therapy is *Client-Centered Therapy: Its Current Practice, Implications and Theory* (Boston: Houghton Mifflin, 1951). His attempt to develop his approach to therapy into a humanistic psychology can be traced in *On Becoming a Person* (Boston: Houghton Mifflin, 1961), *Carl Rogers on Encounter Groups* (New York: Harper & Row, 1970), and *On Personal Power: Inner Strength and Its Revolutionary Impact* (New York: Delacorte Press, 1977). His autobiography is in *A History of Psychology in Autobiography* (New York: Russell, 1968). Howard Kirschenbaum has written a biography called *On Becoming Carl Rogers* (New York: Delacorte Press, 1979). Richard I. Evans has published *Carl Rogers: The Man and His Ideas* (New York: Dutton, 1975), which contains a dialogue with Rogers and a debate between Rogers and Skinner. *Man and the Science of Man* (Columbus, Ohio: Merrill, 1968), edited by W. R. Coulson and Carl Rogers, is a report on a conference where some of the participants were highly critical of humanistic theories.

There have been two editions of Rogers's *Freedom to Learn* (Columbus, Ohio: Merrill, 1969, 1983). A great number of books have recently appeared on the topic of humanistic education. These include The Phi Delta Kappa Symposium on Education Research, *Humanistic Education: Visions and Realities* (Berkeley, Calif.: McCutcheon, 1977); George I. Brown, *Human Teaching for Human Learning* (New York: Viking Press, 1971); Gerald Weinstein and Mario D. Fantini, eds., *Toward Humanistic Education: A Curriculum of Affects* (New York: Praeger, 1970); Donald C. Read and Sidney B. Simon, *Humanistic Education Sourcebook* (Englewood Cliffs, N.J.: Prentice-Hall, 1975).

There is a National Consortium for Humanizing Education located in Dallas, Texas. *The Journal of the Student Personnel Association for Teachers* in 1975 changed its name to *The Humanistic Educator* and publishes articles on theory, research, and application of humanistic education.

INDEX

About the Author

HENRY J. PERKINSON is Professor of Educational History at New York University. A past president of the History of Education Society, he is the author of *The Imperfect Panacea, The Possibilities of Errors, Two Hundred Years of American Educational Thought, Since Socrates,* and other works. His articles have been published in *Harvard Educational Review, History of Education Quarterly, Teachers College Record,* and other periodicals.